L(S

                                                                      T

                                                                      D

To Nigel and Shabs, with whom I share a lot of history.

This revised edition published in 2011 by New Holland Publishers (UK) Ltd

First published in 2008 by New Holland Publishers (UK) Ltd
London • Cape Town • Sydney • Auckland
www.newhollandpublishers.com

Garfield House, 86–88 Edgware Road, London W2 2EA, United Kingdom
80 McKenzie Street, Cape Town 8001, South Africa
Unit 1, 66 Gibbes Street, Chatswood, NSW 2067, Australia
218 Lake Road, Northcote, Auckland, New Zealand

10 9 8 7 6 5 4 3 2 1

A catalogue record for this book is available from the British Library.

ISBN: 978 1 84773 991 9

Publisher: Aruna Vasudevan
Senior Editor: Charlotte Macey
Designer: paul@hellopaul.com
Production: Sarah Kulasek
Picture Research: Jennifer Veall

Reproduction by Pica Digital (Pte) Ltd, Singapore
Printed and bound in Singapore by Tien Wah Press (Pte) Ltd

JOEL LEVY

LOST CITIES
OF THE ANCIENT
WORLD

CONTENTS

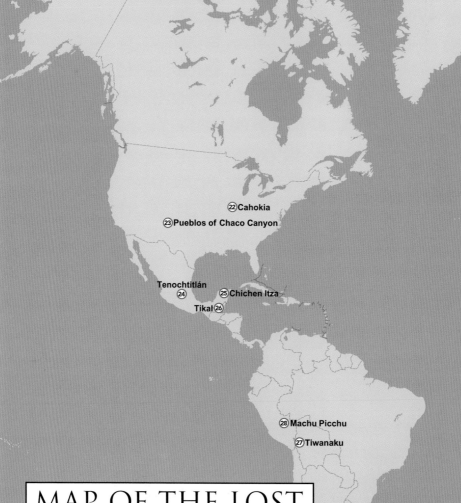

22 Cahokia
23 Pueblos of Chaco Canyon
Tenochtitlán
24
25 Chichen Itza
Tikal 26
28 Machu Picchu
27 Tiwanaku

MAP OF THE LOST CITIES FEATURED IN THIS BOOK

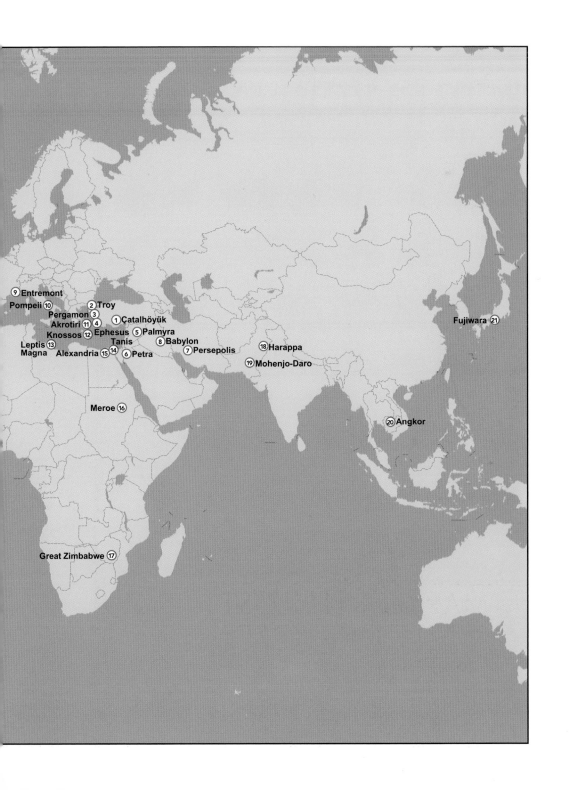

9 Entremont
Pompeii 10
2 Troy
Pergamon 3
Akrotiri 11 4   1 Çatalhöyük
Knossos 12 Ephesus 5 Palmyra
Leptis 13 Tanis
Magna   Alexandria 15 14   6 Petra
8 Babylon
7 Persepolis
18 Harappa
19 Mohenjo-Daro
Fujiwara 21

Meroe 16

20 Angkor

Great Zimbabwe 17

FOREWORD

From the Neolithic to the Middle Ages, from the deserts of Arizona to the plains of Japan – this book tells the stories of lost cities from many different times and places. However, for many of the 'lost cities' described, one or both of the terms could be considered contentious. What constitutes a city, rather than a town or simply a settlement? What does it mean to be 'lost'? For the purposes of covering a wide, varied and interesting range of subjects, both of these terms have been interpreted loosely.

URBAN APOCALYPSE

How do cities become lost? There are really two parts to this question: firstly, why did people stop living in the city? And secondly, how was the physical fabric of the city lost or obscured so that it passed out of knowledge? Perhaps the most straightforward answer to both of these is a sudden disaster – natural or man-made – of some sort. Pompeii and

Akrotiri were both thriving cities until volcanoes erupted nearby. Troy – or at least one phase of its occupation – may have been razed by a horde of Greek invaders. Entremont was besieged and taken by Roman legions, who carried off into slavery most of the residents, returning a few decades later to polish off the remnants. Tenochtitlán was simply replaced by the conquistadors, who constructed a new city in its place.

Beyond this, however, it is possible to identify several factors that can contribute to the decline of a city.

Geographical: cities are founded at particular spots because those places have environmental, strategic or economic advantages, or possibly because they have spiritual significance. If something happens to remove those advantages, the city may lose its raison d'être, and this can be a relatively straightforward reason for urban

Cave tombs at Petra. Once a thriving city because of its favourable location, Petra soon ▶
fell into decline when trade routes redirected the income that had been its lifeblood.

▲ **Chichen Itza.** The greatest city of the northern Maya became a significant city c.600CE, but was razed to the ground following civil war c.1250 CE.

decline. For instance, a city built on a river that changes course or dries up is obviously at risk of losing its economic and environmental underpinnings. Examples of this include Tanis, an ancient Egyptian city built on a branch of the Nile that silted up, and Mohenjo-daro, which suffered when one nearby river changed course and another dried up altogether. Similarly Ephesus was

originally a thriving port city, but is now several kilometres inland. Even in these cases, however, such straightforward physical factors are only part of the story.

Economic: trade routes, like rivers, can change course, and this may affect cities with economic rationales. A good example is Petra, a site originally settled because it combined defensibility with water sources (and possibly for religious reasons), but that flourished because important trade routes passed nearby. When the Romans built a new road that bypassed the city and redirected the bulk of trade, Petra lost its economic basis and slipped into decline. Broader economic factors may also play a part. The decline of Leptis Magna, a Roman port city in North Africa, began with an empire-wide economic crisis in the 3rd century CE.

Environmental: archaeologists and historians are increasingly coming to understand the importance of environmental factors in urban decline. Cities, with their large, high-density populations and hunger for resources – from food and water to firewood, construction materials and raw material for industry – place a heavy load on the environment. Cultures that have lived in a sustainable fashion for millennia can quickly find that their relationship with the environment has changed when they make the shift to urban living. And because environmental collapse can be a very rapid, sudden phenomenon that occurs when certain tipping points are reached, calamity can come upon a city in a very short time, and often just at the exact point when it seems to reach its zenith. The purest examples of this phenomenon are in the Americas, where urban centres such as the Chaco Canyon pueblos and the Classic Mayan cities disturbed relatively fragile ecosystems, tipping them into meltdown with catastrophic consequences for the inhabitants. In the southern lowlands of the Mayan region, it is thought that over a million people probably died and/or emigrated, after 600 years of increasingly magnificent urban achievement collapsed in little over a century. Similar processes may have contributed to the abandonment of cities such as Angkor, Great Zimbabwe and Cahokia. In most cases, natural climate change may also have been involved, with dry periods and droughts exacerbating or triggering environmental collapse.

Political: for much of human history, empires and kingdoms have been ruled by despots and dictators with absolute power. Such individuals are able to found cities by personal decree (albeit for strategic or economic reasons), such as Alexander the Great and Alexandria, Darius the Great and Persepolis and Tenmu and Fujiwara-kyo, but this also means that they can end them in a similar fashion. For instance, when later emperors decided to found a new capital to the north, Fujiwara-kyo was stripped of all useful material and abandoned. Generally, however, political factors work over a longer period and in conjunction with other factors. Alexandria, for instance, suffered a long decline after the Islamic conquest when its new rulers founded a new capital at Cairo. Several other cities, including Tanis, Meroe and Angkor, lost status, power, money and eventually residents to competing cities or when political developments sidelined them.

War: many of the cities described in this book, though not destroyed in a single battle, were tipped into decline by acts of violence. Examples include: Persepolis, according to legend set alight by a vengeful Alexander; Leptis Magna, which never fully recovered from its conquest by Vandals and from an even worse raid by Berbers; and Palmyra, taken by the Romans at the height of its glory.

Exhaustion: sometimes a city can simply become exhausted by a combination of insults and injuries. Babylon, for instance, was among the largest cities in the world for millennia and bounced back from devastating episodes several times in its history, maintaining its pre-eminence through a succession of empires. Finally, however, constant warfare following the collapse of Alexander's short-lived empire drained its human and material resources to the point of no return. Eventually even the irrigation network that enabled the region to support such a large city fell into disrepair. A similar tale of woe bled the life out of Ephesus, once the greatest city in Asia Minor (modern-day Turkey). Between the 7th and 15th centuries CE it was repeatedly assaulted, sacked and otherwise abused, as well as suffering from malaria, coastal retreat and economic breakdown.

CITIES IN PERIL

Many of these factors are still at work today, while new perils increase the risk that the remnants of ancient cities will be irretrievably damaged. Excavation means exposure to the elements and without proper conservation this can spell ruin for ruins, but many of the sites are in countries that cannot afford to pay for conservation. In some areas climate change threatens to exacerbate erosion problems. Quarrying of ruins for bricks and blocks continues at many sites and looting is a growing problem as increasing global affluence increases the market for illegal antiquities. Even today, at supposedly protected sites such as Angkor, gangs of art thieves loot whole façades to order. In a final irony, war once again threatens to raze some ancient cities. The physical fabric of Babylon survived millennia of warfare, yet in recent years massive damage has been inflicted by American troops based on and around the ancient site.

Many of the cities in this book are at risk of being lost all over again, this time forever.

USING THIS BOOK

Lost Cities of the Ancient World is divided into five sections: 'The Near & Middle East', 'Europe', 'Africa', 'South Asia & The Far East' and 'The Americas'.

Each of the 28 lost cities within these sections is introduced with a summary, detailing the modern-day name of the site's location, the dates for when it was constructed and later abandoned, the people who built it and its key features.

It is important to note that the dates for construction and abandonment generally refer to the earliest significant phase of occupation/construction and the latest date of significant occupation. Many sites, however, can trace some form of occupation back to long before the first main phase and in most cases sites were only very gradually abandoned, if at all.

An engaging, in-depth essay covers the known history of the ancient city and its people – sometimes including well-known figures from history, such as Mark Antony or Alexander the Great – and its most important buildings, as well as the story

of its rediscovery and those involved in the excavations. All of this is accompanied by stunning photography of each site and its most famous finds.

Each entry also features practical information, such as transport links and websites, to help you plan how to reach the sites if you choose to (see below), making this not just an essential reference book but also a useful travel guide for history enthusiasts wishing to visit these awe-inspiring sites.

ℹ️ INFORMATION KEY

LOCATION

 Website

TRANSPORT

 Airport

 Train

THE NEAR
& MIDDLE EAST

Cities first appeared in this part of the world in the Neolithic Era, as early as the 8th millennium BCE, heralding the start of civilization in the conventional sense. It is here, in the Near and Middle East, that humans first settled after migrating out of Africa, and that a special convergence of circumstances — including the exploitation of plants and animals that could be domesticated and suitable habitats, and changes in the climate — led hunter–gatherers to become full-time farmers, and later for the farmers to group together in large settlements. And it was in this region that the first urban settlements, such as Çatalhöyük, evolved into the first cities, such as Babylon.

The Near and Middle East were also the theatre for some of the greatest dramas of ancient history, from the superpowers of the Bronze Age to the clashing titans of the Classical Era. This chapter includes some of the most evocative places in history, such as the near-mythical Babylon and the legendary Troy, which tell of great wars and the clash of empires. It also includes some of the most beautiful of ancient cities, such as the rock-hewn delights of Petra and the graceful columns of Palmyra.

This region has an unequalled variety and wealth of history and the cities covered reflect this, spanning a stretch of time from the Neolithic Era to Late Antiquity, taking in empires and civilizations from ancient Assyrians and the Achaemenids to the Greeks and Romans. Some of the cities, such as Petra and Palmyra, reflect the status of this region as the crossroads of history, their architecture combining elements from Mediterranean and Middle Eastern cultures. Others define the styles of their respective cultures, whether at Babylon, where many of the idioms of the city were invented, or at Pergamum, where the Classical city attained perhaps its fullest ideal.

The Monastery at Petra. A rock-cut tomb that probably dates back to the 1st century CE but which may have been used as a church by Byzantine monks, hence the name. Visible in the centre of the pediment is a giant urn, a characteristic feature of Nabataean architecture. ▶

ÇATALHÖYÜK

See map p.7   1

LOCATION:	CENTRAL TURKEY
CONSTRUCTED:	*c.*7400BCE
ABANDONED:	*c.*6000BCE
BUILT BY:	NEOLITHIC HUNTER–GATHERER FARMERS
KEY FEATURES:	NO STREETS; SUB-FLOOR BURIALS; INTERIOR DECORATION, MURALS AND FIGURINES

Çatalhöyük is a Neolithic settlement of almost unprecedented size, with many remarkable features – from its close-packed layout to the wealth of art and symbolism that adorns its walls.

In the Konya Basin area of Anatolia, in central Turkey, two mounds rise above the semi-arid plain, separated by the course of the now extinct Carsamba River. This is the site of Çatalhöyük, Turkish for 'fork-mound', named for a path that forked when it reached the base of the larger mound, Çatalhöyük East. In the Neolithic Era, from 7400–6000BCE, this was a settlement of up to 8,000 people living in 2,000 houses, covering over 12.25 hectares (30 acres). Two principal digs – the excavations of James Mellaart in the late 1950s and early 60s, and the ongoing excavations under Ian Hodder since the 1990s – have uncovered some unusual features at the site

THE TOWN WITH NO STREETS

The most striking feature of Çatalhöyük was that it had no streets. The houses were packed so close together that they effectively formed a single solid mass and access to each house and travel around the town was via the rooftops. The buildings themselves were rectangular, 11–48 square metres (118–517 square feet) in area and probably one-storey high. They were constructed from mud bricks with wooden posts as roof supports, with flat roofs of wooden beams on top of which bundles of reed were laid and mud was packed on top.

The 'Leopard Queen'. This sculpture of a woman sitting on a chair, flanked by leopards ▶ was found in a grain bin. It may have been placed here to encourage fertility.

▲ **Excavation.** The current excavations under Ian Hodder have identified at least 80 different buildings.

Everything was covered with a lime-rich plaster, including internal features of the houses such as ovens, platforms and shelves. A small square opening in the south side of the roof led into the house via a wooden stairway of squared timber. This gave access to the main room, where most of the domestic activity took place. Smaller rooms led off the main room and were accessed by low doorways; they were probably used for storage. There were no windows or side doors.

The oven or hearth was situated beneath the ceiling opening to allow smoke to escape. Ash and debris scraped out of the oven made the floor area in this part of the room relatively dirty. It was separated from cleaner zones of the room by ridges in the floor or by raised platforms, which might be used for sleeping or other purposes. Some were covered with reed mats. In fine weather most activity probably took place on the town's roofs, but during the bitterly cold winters families would have huddled in their smoke-filled houses. The bodies of Çatalhöyük residents reveal deposits of soot along their ribs. This is soot that had accumulated in their lungs from lifetimes of exposure to smoke-filled interiors and that settled onto the ribs as the lung tissue decomposed after death.

THE ANCESTORS BELOW

Another striking feature of Çatalhöyük was that its inhabitants buried their dead directly beneath their living-room floors. The area around the hearth was used for burying babies and also for storing caches of obsidian (see page 20), with hollow spaces for pots or other small items. Beneath the raised platforms, however, the bodies of older children and adults were buried, usually wrapped in reed mats or placed in baskets.

After a certain period of time – perhaps if a house became decrepit or enough people had been buried in it – the inhabitants would rebuild over the original on the same floor plan. The existing building would be cut down to a height of around 1 metre (3¼ feet) and then carefully filled in. Ritual or talismanic objects were sometimes deliberately placed among the filling material. Then the new house would be raised on top of this foundation. In this way the inhabitants of Çatalhöyük could live in close connection with their ancestors going back centuries, with the rising settlement mound – that reached up to 20 metres (65½ feet) above the surrounding plain with 18 levels of habitation – representing the physical embodiment of their group identity and sociocultural values.

LEOPARDS AND BULLS

The third remarkable feature of Çatalhöyük is the extensive art and symbolism found in the form of its murals and figurines. The prehistoric residents covered their white plaster interiors with a variety of murals, including abstract patterns, such as circles, and colourful and exciting hunting scenes. These include many scenes of men (their gender indicated by their ithyphallic appearance – shown with erect penises – and occasionally by a beard) hunting or sporting with wild animals such as aurochs (giant prehistoric cattle) and leopards. By contrast there are no depictions of farming. Perhaps the most famous mural dates from c.6500BCE and appears to show a view of the town with the nearby twin-peaked volcano of Hasan Dagˇi in the background; if the interpretation is correct, the mural is the oldest map and/ or landscape painting ever discovered.

Other interior decoration included horns of animals mounted on the walls and skulls of animals (and possibly ancestors), remodelled with clay and painted. Some figurines have been recovered from beneath floors and in filled-in rooms. They come in a variety of forms, including animals, non-gender specific humans and, in the upper, later levels of occupation, voluptuous women. A famous example, found in a grain bin where it may have been placed to enhance fertility, is of a voluptuous woman seated on a chair or throne, flanked by a pair of leopards (see page 17).

LIFE IN ÇATALHÖYÜK

The people of Çatalhöyük had Stone Age technology. They utilized obsidian (volcanic glass) to make a variety of sharp and functional tools, and also made pottery, wove fabric and had other skills. They had basic agriculture, which became more important to them over the lifetime of the town, and supplemented their diet with hunting and the gathering of wild foods. The area around Çatalhöyük was marshy, providing good water resources and fish and game, as well as the mud and reeds they used for construction.

Each building probably housed a family of between five and ten people, and in fine weather most of their activities would have taken place on the town roofs. Men and women probably shared tasks such as pottery and obsidian tool making, which

▼ **Child burial.** This child's skeleton was found buried with necklaces and ornaments.

together with agriculture were the main industries of the town, giving them products they could trade for timber from the nearby hills, for the raw obsidian from Cappadocia about 145 kilometres (90 miles) away, and even for goods from much further afield, such as baskets from Mesopotamia and shells from the Red Sea. Rubbish from each household, including faecal matter, was simply dumped into the spaces around and between buildings, so that they became effectively embedded in a giant midden pile. Ash from the fires and ovens helped to sterilize this waste, but even so there must have been considerable stench and vermin issues.

Today the mound of Çatalhöyük shows two peaks, suggesting that in ancient times the town actually consisted of two slightly separate built-up areas. This is consistent with an endogamous culture – one where people marry only within the group, tribe or in this case, settlement. Many such societies are actually split into two sub-groups or tribes, which intermarry (to prevent incestuous marriage), and this may be what is indicated by the twin peaks of the mound. The lack of evidence of any contemporary settlements in the area further suggests that kinship and marriage were heavily localized.

Ian Hodder questions whether Çatalhöyük can be seen as a city in the proper sense of the word, because its layout and the uniformity of the buildings indicate that there were few or no public spaces or buildings, no central focus, such as a palace or temple, and no evidence of a social hierarchy or specialization of employment. It seems that each household was responsible for and to itself and there is no sign that they formed a township for defensive reasons. The exact reason why they did gather at Çatalhöyük remains a mystery, as do the causes of the town's abandonment in around 6000BCE. A smaller settlement to the west of the main site was briefly occupied from about 6000–5700BCE. Did the inhabitants of Çatalhöyük proper simply move, and if so, why?

ⓘ information

Location
Çatalhöyük
South-east of Konya
Turkey

 Research site
www.catalhoyuk.com

Transport
 Konya

TROY

See map p.7 ②

LOCATION:	DARDANELLES, TURKEY
CONSTRUCTED:	c.2600BCE
ABANDONED:	ROMAN TIMES
BUILT BY:	TROJANS? SUBKINGDOM OF HITTITE EMPIRE?
KEY FEATURES:	NUMEROUS PHASES OF OCCUPATION; MASSIVE WALLS AND CITADEL; TREASURE OF PRIAM

For the ancient Greeks and Romans there was no doubt that Troy was a real place and that the epics of the Greek poet Homer were genuine records of history, but with the rise of critical history in the modern era, Troy was consigned to the realm of legend.

Homer's celebrated epic poems, the *Iliad* and *Odyssey*, give a clear picture of a great city situated on a hill near the mouth of the River Scamander in a region known as Troas (modern-day Çanakkale in Turkey), a city known both as Troy and as Ilion. Legendary Troy commanded the trade routes between the Aegean and the Black Sea via the Straits of the Dardanelles, and ruled over the surrounding lands from behind its apparently unbreachable walls.

◀ **Excavation at Hissarlik.** Heinrich Schliemann discovered the remains of several ancient cities buried on top of one another at Hissarlik.

Ancient Greek historians dated the decade-long Trojan War to between the 14th and 12th centuries BCE, most popularly to 1193–1183BCE, at the culmination of which Troy was destroyed and the Trojans scattered, their lands eventually occupied by later immigrants. To the Greeks of Homer's age (8th century BCE) the ruins of the ancient city were still visible and the remnants of the walls may even have been used for protection by the small remaining community. Alexander the Great visited it in 334BCE and the Roman emperor Augustus founded a city there called Novum Ilium (New Troy), which flourished for 300 years but declined under the Byzantine Empire. By the time of the Islamic conquest, the city was deserted and the location lost. Thanks to Homer, ancient Troy was never forgotten, but European intellectuals assumed that the stories were little more than myths.

HEINRICH SCHLIEMANN

One man who disagreed was German businessman and amateur archaeologist Heinrich Schliemann. Fascinated by Troy since he was a little boy, Schliemann had made a fortune trading in Russia and America and decided to devote himself to tracking down proof of the existence of Homer's Troy. Homer's epics contain specific geographical information and although the coastline in the region has changed over the millennia some of these clues pointed to a mound near a village called Hissarlik. In 1870, Schliemann started digging and quickly discovered that the mound concealed evidence of several ancient cities built on top of one another.

Convinced that he had found the site of Troy, but with little patience for the painstaking methods of conventional archaeology, Schliemann had his workmen dig a trench right down to the lowest and oldest phase, which he assumed must be the original Troy of Homer. In doing so, he ploughed through no fewer than eight other phases of occupation, doing so much damage that some contemporaries called him 'the second destroyer of Troy'.

Eventually Schliemann decided that the penultimate phase of occupation, labelled Troy II (Troy I being the oldest and IX the youngest), which had massive stone walls and towers and grand public buildings, must be the city of Priam and Paris. A layer of ash separating this phase from the next indicated that the city had perished in fire, matching Homer's description of the demise of Troy.

Reports of Schliemann's discovery captured global attention, but the best was yet to come. In 1873, he unearthed a bronze vessel from the walls of a building he assumed to be Priam's palace, which proved to contain a fabulous treasure of gold and silver, including exotic headdresses and beads, plates and drinking vessels.

Archaeologists who succeeded Schliemann discovered that some of his primary conclusions were off the mark. Troy II was quickly identified as an early Bronze Age town dating back to 2600–2250BCE, more than a thousand years before the supposed time of Priam. The other phases of note were Troy VI – a high Bronze Age citadel with huge walls and palacelike buildings and Troy VII, its successor, which are considered much more likely candidates for the Homeric city. Troy IX was Novum Ilium, the city founded by the Romans.

TROY VI

The most impressive ruins at the site are from the phase named Troy VI, which dates to the mid-2nd millennium BCE. Imposing fortifications, with massive walls of dressed limestone blocks topped with mud bricks,

over 4 metres (13¼ feet) thick, and
five gates protected by high towers,
encircled a citadel area containing
concentric rings of large buildings
on mounting terraces. Some of
these buildings are two storeys high,
made of wood and bricks on stone
foundations, and may have been
palaces or mansions. Clearly Troy VI
was a centre of economic and military
importance, although the fortified
area was more of a citadel than a city.
In 1988, however, further excavations
revealed evidence of city ramparts
enclosing a much larger area, allowing
space for up to 10,000 inhabitants.

So was Troy VI the Troy of Homer? For
a while it was thought likely, but Troy VI
probably dates to 1800–1300BCE, outside
most of the traditional dates ascribed to
Homeric Troy. More importantly, there are
none of the telltale signs of war or siege,
such as ash from fires, buried stores or
treasure, goods abandoned by fleeing
residents or the skeletons of those killed
violently. The city was probably destroyed
by an earthquake.

TROY VIIA

Many of the signs of war are present in
the next phase of occupation, known as
Troy VIIa (because it is the first of several
sub-phases of occupation). Troy VIIa was

▲ **Golden death mask.** Discovered by Heinrich
Schliemann in 1873 at the Hissarlik excavation.
He claimed that it was the 'Mask of Agamemnon'.

essentially the same city as Troy VI,
apparently reoccupied and partially rebuilt
after the earthquake. The evidence suggests
that conditions had changed, however,
with some of the grand mansions of the
earlier phase now subdivided for multiple
occupancy and the damaged fortifications
of previous eras merely patched up, rather
than enlarged/improved as past generations
of Trojans had done. The new buildings
were more densely packed and smaller
(possibly indicating that people who used
to live in the wider metropolis were now
crowded into the citadel for safety).

▲ **The Amphitheatre.** This venue was created during the Roman phase of settlement at Troy, when the city was known as Novum Ilium (Troy IX).

Many houses have storage pits for large clay jars built into their floors, possibly for supplies in case of siege (although this may also just have been normal practice), and some unburied skeletons have been found. Most significantly, the demise of the city is marked with a layer of ash. Troy VIIa dates to around 1250BCE, and although there is significant debate over the exact date of its destruction, it was probably around 1200BCE, similar to Classical Greek dating of the Trojan War.

WILUSA OF THE HITTITES
Important evidence apparently linking the city at Hissarlik to Homer's epic poems comes from the records of the Hittites, the civilization under whose remit the region of Troas would have fallen in the late 13th century BCE. Hittite texts mention the place-names Wilusa and Taruisa. Mycenaean Greeks used a 'w' letter that later Greeks dropped, and evidence from the meter used in the composition of the *Iliad* suggests that Ilion was originally Willion, probably a derivation of Wilusa. Taruisa, meanwhile,

is lexically linked to Troas and Troy. Other texts describe features of Wilusa, such as a water tunnel, which conform to archaeological findings at Hissarlik. Hittite diplomatic letters mention an incident involving Wilusa and aggression by a nation called the Ahhiyawa, possibly a Hittite version of the Achaeans.

HOMER'S TROY?

Troy VIIa thus seems like the most likely candidate as the true Homeric city, but there is controversy over whether the evidence really points to this conclusion, and even over whether there is any historical accuracy to the epics. The Hittite textual evidence is circumstantial and there is no direct evidence linking the site at Hissarlik to Wilusa or the place names Ilion or Troy. In fact, some scholars suggest that there never was a city called Troy and that the ancients mistook the name of a region (Troas) for the name of a city.

What about Homer's apparent accuracy regarding the geography of Troy/Hissarlik?

Recent research on the ancient coastline of the area (before sedimentation) suggests that it closely matches Homer's description, as do other features of Hissarlik. But this could simply reflect the fact that Homer travelled to the area before composing his epics. The Greeks had not long before settled nearby areas, and it is possible that they sought out a place to which they could attach pre-existing legends and folklore.

If Homer was right, the Achaeans who destroyed Troy were Bronze Age Greeks, i.e. Mycenaeans. Certainly the linguistic evidence of the epics suggests that they derive from Mycenaean legends and traditions, but there is no evidence linking the destruction of Troy to the Mycenaeans. In fact, archaeologists believe that at the period in question, around 1200BCE, the Mycenaeans might well have been preoccupied with the collapse of their civilization in its heartland in Greece.

What the excavations at Hissarlik do prove is that this was the site of an important city for 2,000 years, the centre of a fascinating, yet mysterious culture.

---

 information

Location

Troy (Truva)
North-western Turkey

 Travel site
www.turkeytravelplanner.com/go/Aegean/Troy

Transport

 Çanakkale

PERGAMUM

See map p.7 ③

LOCATION:	NORTH-WESTERN TURKEY, NEAR THE AEGEAN COAST
CONSTRUCTED:	c.300BCE
ABANDONED:	c.8TH CENTURY CE
BUILT BY:	ATTALID GREEKS
KEY FEATURES:	ALTAR OF ZEUS; LIBRARY OF PERGAMUM; ASKLEPIEION; AMPHITHEATRE; TRAJANEUM

Pergamum was an ancient Greek city state in Mysia, in north-western Anatolia (modern-day Turkey), which came to rival Athens and Alexandria as centres of Hellenistic achievement and renown. The city was based around an acropolis built on a 355-metre (1,165-feet) high spur between two tributaries of the River Caicus (today known as Bakırçay).

It was a minor settlement until the early 3rd century BCE, when Lysimachus made it a fortress for the safeguarding of his treasury. Lysimachus had been one of Alexander the Great's generals and had taken control of Anatolia following Alexander's death. Lysimachus contended with Seleucus of Syria for control of Asia Minor and was eventually killed by his eastern rival in 281BCE (at the battle of Corupedium). Philataerus, the man Lysimachus had appointed to control

the fortress, seized control of the treasury and established a power base at Pergamum.

THE ATTALIDS

Philataerus established the Attalid dynasty, named after his father Attalus. His successor, Eumenes, secured the city, but it was his nephew Attalus I (269–197BCE) who achieved eternal renown for Pergamum by defeating the Galatians – Celts from Thrace who had crossed over to Asia Minor in 278BCE and terrorized the Greek states of the region with decades of raids and plundering.

ROMAN PERGAMUM

Attalus III had no heir. To avoid civil conflict over the succession he bequeathed the

The Trajaneum. A temple devoted to the cult of the ▶ Emperor Trajan on the Pergamene Acropolis.

▲ **The Acropolis.** This citadel was home to all of the important buildings in Pergamum, including temples to the Roman emperors; the library; the Altar of Zeus; the agora and the amphitheatre.

kingdom to Rome. On his death in 133BCE, there was a brief uprising, but this was crushed by the Roman army. On the whole, the Romans respected Pergamene property and autonomy, making the city the capital of the province of Asia Minor. In recognition of its influence and status the city was granted permission to build temples to the imperial cult, including ones in honour of Augustus and Trajan.

THE ACROPOLIS

The important buildings of Pergamum were grouped together on the acropolis, which extended down the sides of the steep central hill. At the top were the king's palaces and the arsenals (barracks and military storehouses). Descending the hill from west to east, lower terraces housed the *temenos* or sacred precinct, which included temples to the Roman emperors,

long. Other features of the Acropolis include the *heroons*, or royal tombs, and the Propylea, or monumental gate.

Below the Acropolis was a gymnasium – a centre for the physical, intellectual and moral training of the city's youth. Measuring 200 x 150 metres (656 x 492 feet), it was the largest gymnasium in the Greek world, reflecting the importance of education to the Attalids (they also sponsored educational establishments in other Greek cities as a way of boosting their profile and status). It had three levels, each assigned to a different age group, with exercise yards, a lecture hall, its own library, baths and a temple. From the lower levels of the city a sacred way ran off to the south-west, towards the Asklepieion (see page 33).

THE ALTAR AND OTHER TEMPLES

Pergamum hosted temples to the cult of Augustus and Trajan. Building such temples had financial and political benefits, attracting patronage from emperors and fostering closer ties with Rome. To the south of the acropolis, in the main town, was a Serapeum – a temple to the Egyptian god Serapis, which later became the site of a Christian church known as the 'Red Basilica'. The Christian community at Pergamum was one of the Seven Churches of Asia to which the Book of Revelation was addressed.

then the famous library (see page 32) and its associated Sanctuary of Athena, then the Altar of Zeus (see page 32) and below that the agora (forum/marketplace). In front of these, facing south over the plain and still dominating the prospect of the city today, a great amphitheatre with seating for 10,000 people was cut into the steep hillside. Next to it was a temple to Dionysus, god of wine and entertainment, while running along its base was a giant *stoa* (pillared portico) 247 metres (810 feet)

The most famous religious building in Pergamum, however, is no longer there, having been removed by German archaeologists between 1879 and 1904. This is the Altar of Zeus, also known as the Pergamon Altar, now housed in the Pergamon Museum in Berlin. Erected by Eumenes II after victorious campaigns against the Galatians, it commemorated his father's famous defeat of the same foes, although it also encoded a wider message about Pergamum's status in the Greek world. It was a stepped square podium mounted to a terrace with a central altar surrounded by a colonnade, upon which was mounted a huge 113-metre (371-feet) long frieze of the war between the Olympian gods and the Titans, along with other mythological scenes. After the sculptures of Phidias from the Parthenon, this frieze is considered to be the highest achievement of Classical Greek sculpture.

THE LIBRARY

Pergamum's primacy attracted many scholars, poets, philosophers and scientists,

▼ **The Amphitheatre.** Sited in front of the Acropolis, this theatre had seating for 10,000 spectators.

and the Attalids themselves were keen collectors of scrolls and books. The centre of this intellectual activity was the Library of Pergamum, second only to its fierce rival the Library of Alexandria. Ancient writers claimed that it housed 200,000 scrolls, although this is probably a substantial exaggeration, with the existing ruins suggesting a more modest 17,000. The library included reading rooms and document storage shelves, and was said to have a built-in air conditioning system of vents to help keep the scrolls and books dry. Supposedly it met its demise when Mark Antony had the entire collection removed and given as a wedding gift to Cleopatra, to replenish the Library of Alexandria.

THE ASKLEPIEION

A few kilometres to the south of the main city was the Asklepieion, a sort of spa–hospital complex, including a temple to Asklepios – the Greek god of healing, baths, apartments, a theatre,

---

DREAM INCUBATION

A core element of ancient therapies was the procedure of dream incubation, for which patients would pray to the gods of healing for help with an ailment and then sleep in one of the specially provided apartments or cells. Under the influence of the tutelary spirits of the Asklepieion, the patients would have dreams of a diagnostic and therapeutic nature, with priest–physicians on hand to help analyze and interpret them.

---

treatment rooms, a library, as well as a dream incubation facility (see box above). Developed to its fullest extent under the Romans, especially Hadrian, the Asklepieion was considered one of the wonders of the Roman world, attracting patients and scholars from far and wide, including famous names such as the orator Aelius Aristides and Galen (the 2nd-century CE Pergamene physician whose works formed the basis of Western medicine for the next 1,600 years).

---

information

Location

Pergamum (Bergama)
Izmir Province
Turkey

 Travel site
www.sacred-destinations.
com/turkey/pergamum

Transport

 Izmir

EPHESUS

See map p.7 (**4**)

LOCATION: AEGEAN COAST OF TURKEY
CONSTRUCTED: 10TH CENTURY BCE
ABANDONED: c.15TH CENTURY CE
BUILT BY: GREEK COLONISTS
KEY FEATURES: ARTEMISION; ODEON; LIBRARY
OF CELSUS; GREAT THEATRE;
BATHS OF CONSTANTINE; STATUES
OF THE AMAZONS

Eighteen hundred years ago, Ephesus was the greatest city in Asia Minor, the richest port in the Roman Empire and the site of the Temple of Artemis, a cult site of extreme antiquity and one of the Seven Wonders of the Ancient World.

CITY OF THE AMAZONS

The city had been founded by Athenian and Ionian Greek colonists in around the 10th century BCE on the site of an older Hittite settlement called Apasa. Low hills surrounded by fertile though marshy plains commanded the course of the River Cayster or Kaystros (*Küçük Menderes* in modern-day Turkish) where it flowed into the Aegean, and it was here that the Greeks built their city.

The colony prospered, producing some of the first coins ever minted, c. 700BCE, but in the 7th century BCE it was sacked by rampaging Cimmerians who burned down the Artemision (Temple of Artemis). Later it fell into Lydian hands when it was besieged by King Croesus. He used his legendary wealth to help rebuild the Artemision. When Cyrus of Persia conquered Lydia in 547BCE, Ephesus fell under Persian dominion, but the Persian emperors, out of respect for the temple, left it unmolested. In 334BCE, the city welcomed Alexander the Great, who re-established its democratic government, and it then passed into the control of his general Lysimachus, who relocated many of the inhabitants and enclosed the city within a defensive wall.

◀ **Library of Celsus.** The partially restored façade of the Library of Celsus, the most impressive ruin in Ephesus. The library held a collection of 12,000 scrolls.

ROMAN AND BYZANTINE EPHESUS

Lysimachus was defeated by the Seleucids, but they in turn gave way to the Romans who handed the city over to Pergamum (see page 28), although in 133BCE it returned to Roman control. Under the Romans Ephesus vied with Pergamum for the status of chief city of Asia, eventually becoming the capital of the province of Asia, while its mercantile activities made it for a while the richest port in the empire. Roman control of Ephesus continued unbroken except for the uprising of Mithridates VI of Pontus in 88BCE. Corrupt Roman tax farmers and speculators had aroused the ire of the Asians and Mithridates incited the Asian cities to rise up against their Roman overlords and massacre every Latin in Asia. Even those who tried to claim sanctuary at the Artemision (see page 38) were slaughtered. Estimates of the death toll range from 80–150,000. When the Roman general Sulla defeated Mithridates and crushed the uprising, Ephesus escaped with a heavy fine.

From the 1st century CE Ephesus flourished, growing to around 225,000 inhabitants (some authorities claim it was much larger, with up to 500,000 inhabitants, which would probably have made it the largest city in the world at the time). Many impressive buildings were constructed and the city was provided with some of the most extensive aqueducts and other hydrological infrastructure of the ancient world. The Artemision, too, continued to flourish, although it became a focus of discontent for the growing Christian community. Ephesus was to become one of the most important dioceses of the nascent Church, with cult sites such as the tomb of St John the Apostle and the last resting place of the Virgin Mary. Major church councils were held there, but eventually it lost influence to Constantinople.

Under the Byzantines the city declined, its population reduced by malaria from the surrounding marshes and its fabric degraded by a series of assaults and sackings: by the Arabs in 655 and 717; the Iconoclasts in the 8th and 9th centuries; the Seljuk Turks in 1090 and the early 14th century; Catalonian mercenaries in the pay of Byzantium; then the Turks again; Tamerlane in 1403; and a series of feuding emirs throughout the rest of the 15th century.

MAIN BUILDINGS OF EPHESUS

Excavations by mainly British and Austrian archaeologists have revealed some of the splendour of ancient Ephesus. Paved streets (some paved with marble, others with mosaics) and colonnades lead to some impressive surviving or rebuilt structures. The odeon was a roofed theatre used for musical performances, poetry readings and prize-giving; it had seating for 2,200 people. Next to it was the agora or public square, with large halls, columns, porticoes and shops. Curetes Street runs west from here to the town centre, close to which is the most impressive extant façade in Ephesus – the Library of Celsus. Built to honour the recently deceased proconsul of Asia, T. Julius Celsus, whose tomb lies nearby, this library held 12,000 scrolls. Ingenious architecture, involving a convex lower tier, makes the façade seem bigger than it really is.

From the centre of town the Sacred Way, also known as the Marble Street, leads to the Great Theatre, which has seating for 25,000. A broad road known as Arcadiane ran from here to the port, passing on the right the great Baths of Constantine, which were so large that visitors would sometimes mistake them for the Artemision. In the north-west of the ancient city lay the Double Church of the Virgin and St John, where the early church councils were held.

▼ **Street mosaic.** The tiled streets at Ephesus are symbolic of the extraordinary wealth of the city.

▲ **The Great Theatre at Ephesus.** This venue was built primarily in the 1st century AD and used until the 5th century.

THE ARTEMISION

The ancient Greek writer Antipater of Thessalonica wrote that although he had seen the Hanging Gardens of Babylon, the Colossus of Rhodes, the Mausoleum and the Pyramids, none compared to the glories of the Artemision, 'when I saw the house of Artemis that mounted to the clouds, those other marvels lost their brilliancy, and I said, "Lo, apart from Olympus, the Sun never looked on aught so grand."'

The colossal temple was rebuilt several times. It was relatively small (originally just an altar on a platform of green schist) until Croesus paid for a huge Ionic temple, built entirely of marble and incorporating 127 columns. This incarnation of the temple was 116 metres (380½ feet) long and 55 metres (180½ feet) wide, covering an area of about 7,430 square metres (79,975 square feet). According to Pliny, it was built on marshy ground to help protect it from earthquakes and took 120 years to complete, finally being consecrated sometime between 430 and 420 BCE. Among the many treasures with which it was endowed were a series of bronze statues of Amazons created for a competition by the leading sculptors of the day, including Phidias, who made the famous chryselephantine statues of Zeus and Athena Parthenos.

According to the ancient scribes, this version of the temple was destroyed in 356 BCE (on the same night as the birth of Alexander the Great), when a man named Herostratus set fire to the wooden frame of the roof, hoping to win eternal renown for his evil deed. It was soon rebuilt, this time with columns 18 metres (59 feet) high and continued to attract crowds of pilgrims, priests and hangers-on, generating considerable industry for the city. A coin from the reign of Claudius (c. 50CE) shows the temple pediment with three windows or openings, which were probably used to display either the famous bronze Amazons or images of the goddess Artemis. But the version of Artemis worshipped at Ephesus was very different from that of Athens or the Roman Diana. The Ephesian Artemis–Cybele combined prehistoric traditions with Persian and other influences, to produce a complex iconography featuring a woman with many breasts (that may actually have symbolized eggs, bees or the testicles of sacrificial bulls).

An important feature of the temple was the right to asylum that applied within its sacred bounds, which meant that criminals, fugitives and those in fear of their lives could not be harmed or arrested once they passed within its precincts. Under Mark Antony the boundaries of asylum were extended to include parts of the city proper, which resulted in that quarter degenerating into a den of vice. The inviolate nature of the sacred precincts also made the Artemision a safe place to store money, and great quantities of treasure were banked here.

Although it was sacked and burned by the Goths in 262CE, it was at least partially restored and continued to be a major religious centre until the Edict of Theodosius forced the closing of the pagan temples, and its stones were quarried for the construction of a nearby cathedral. Some were even burnt for lime. By the time of the Ottoman conquest the site was buried under 1 metre (3¼ feet) of silt, and today a single forlorn pillar marks the spot where this ancient wonder once stood.

 ## information

Location

Ephesus
Selcuk
Western Turkey

 Travel site
www.sacred-destinations.com/turkey/ephesus

Transport

 Izmir

PALMYRA

See map p.7 ⑤

LOCATION:	CENTRAL SYRIA
CONSTRUCTED:	*c.*330BCE
ABANDONED:	*c.*6TH CENTURY CE
BUILT BY:	PALMYRENES
KEY FEATURES:	TARIFF OF PALMYRA; TEMPLE OF BEL; PROPYLEA; THEATRE; COLUMNS; DIOCLETIAN BATHS; HYBRID CULTURAL INFLUENCES

The ruins of ancient Palmyra are among the world's most impressive remnants of lost cities. Graceful columns of rose-hued stone soar into the desert sky along colonnaded streets, recalling the city's former elegance. Yet appearances might be regarded as deceptive, for the animating impulses of Palmyra were trade and money rather than art or culture.

Palmyra is the Greek name for the city of Tadmor, probably derived from the Semitic word for 'palm tree'. Known as the Bride of the Desert, Palmyra was an oasis city in the centre of Syria, 215 kilometres (133½ miles) north-east of Damascus. It lay on the border between the semi-arid Badiya, or Syrian steppe, and the wide expanse of desert that separates it from the upper reaches of the Euphrates. The city's form and culture were a classic marriage of East and West, with Hellenistic and Roman influences melded to Arabic, Egyptian, Mesopotamian and Persian ones. What you can see today is effectively a snapshot of a Roman city frozen at the height of the empire's glory.

MERCHANT CITY

Biblical tradition attributes the founding of Tadmor to Solomon (*c.*1000BCE), but it is extremely unlikely that Hebrew kings ever ruled this region, while Assyrian inscriptions on tablets found at the ancient city of Mari on the Euphrates dating back to *c.*1800BCE, show that a settlement had existed there since the Bronze Age. Hot springs provided a constant supply of water, attracting caravans crossing the arid wastes between the Euphrates – which gave access

Gracious colonnades. Ancient Palmyra, with the Arab fort of Qalaat ibn Ma'an in the background. ▶

to the trade of Persia, the Gulf of Arabia, India and China and the Silk Road – and Damascus and the west. But at this point, it may have been little more than a tent city.

According to some sources, Alexander the Great and his successors, the Seleucids, founded a more permanent city and gave it a Hellenistic constitution, but even in 41BCE, when Mark Antony led a cavalry raid across the desert to plunder its riches, Palmyra's inhabitants were sufficiently mobile to have vacated the city along with all their movable goods (having received advanced warning of his attack). It was officially absorbed into the Roman province of Syria in 17CE, and Roman influence was to make the city one of the richest in the Near East.

The heyday of Palmyra came in the 2nd century CE when Roman road building caused a major shift in the trade routes, and an increasing quantity of merchandise that had previously flowed through Petra (see page 47) now travelled via Palmyra. The city's prosperity was cemented when the Roman emperor Hadrian visited in 129CE, granting Palmyra 'free city' status, with attendant financial and regulatory benefits, after which it became known as Hadriana Palmyra. Later the city was made capital of the Roman province of Syria Phoenice. At its peak, there were some 30,000 inhabitants.

In 217CE, the city received a further boost from the part-Syrian emperor Caracalla, who awarded it official 'colony' status, which exempted it from imperial taxes. Palmyra was now at the height of its prosperity. Grand civic buildings in the Roman style were complemented by great temples, rich merchant's mansions and elaborate tombs. Pillars and inscriptions have preserved important information about this era, illustrating how trade was the lifeblood of the city.

The famous Tariff of Palmyra is an inscription from around 137CE, setting out financial and tax laws, detailing the commodities that passed through Palmyra and the levels of taxes and duties levied on them. As well as taxes on goods from ivory and silk to precious gems and spices, the tariff also records levies on other commodities and commercial activities from water to prostitution. The city's financial authority – known as the 'treasurers' – were as or more important than its civic governance and were actively involved in helping to set up and even fund trade ventures. Large camel trains, for instance, which might be beyond the means of an individual merchant or even a group of merchants, would be underwritten by the city itself. The city's mercantile reach extended as far as the Mediterranean and the Indian Ocean, where ships owned by Palmyrenes plied the waters off Italy and controlled the silk trade from the Far East.

▲ **Amphitheatre.** The impressive remains of the Roman amphitheatre at Palmyra **c.**1st century CE.

QUEEN ZENOBIA

Although Palmyra was now an official Roman colony, it remained very much on the borders of the empire, a useful buffer between Rome and its eastern rivals, the Parthians. When the Romans were succeeded as masters of Persia and Mesopotamia by the Sassanids in the 3rd century CE, however, trouble began to brew. In 227CE, the Sassanids closed their end of the caravan routes, dealing a heavy blow to Palmyran trade. Over the next few decades, Rome and the Sassanids clashed repeatedly, culminating in 259CE with the capture of the Roman emperor Valerian and the loss of significant territory.

At this time, the ruler of Palmyra was a local prince, Septimus Odaenathus, whom the Romans had appointed governor of Syria Phoenice; it was to him that Rome turned to avenge their losses. Vigorous campaigning saw him regain much of the lost territory and in 260CE he was recognized by Rome as Corrector Totius Orientis – Governor of all the East. But Odaenathus had greater ambitions. He proclaimed himself king and

▲ **Temple of Bel.** Palmyra's main temple displays a mixture of influences, including Greek, Roman and Semitic.

later emperor, but in 267CE he was assassinated in mysterious circumstances and his wife, Queen Zenobia, took over the regency on behalf of their infant son.

Zenobia proved to be one of the most remarkable women in history. Of mixed Greek–Arab descent she was renowned for her beauty and intelligence. Well educated and fluent in several languages, she attracted philosophers, artists and poets to her court, but was also renowned as a superb horsewoman and a capable general. Under her rule, Palmyra briefly flowered into an empire as she took advantage of Roman

weakness to conquer the Levant, Egypt and much of Asia Minor. But her career as empress was short lived. Emperor Aurelian marshalled his legions, reconquered the lost territories and besieged Zenobia at Palmyra in 272CE. Eventually she was captured and taken as a prisoner to be paraded through the streets of Rome in golden chains, along with her son. Accounts of her end are varied – in some versions she committed suicide or was beheaded, while in others Diocletian gave her a villa in Tivoli and she married a senator and became a popular fixture of Roman society.

The Romans never forgave Palmyra, especially after the city again rebelled in 273CE, and it was looted and razed. Later, the emperor Diocletian made it a garrison town, but it never recovered its glory. Under the Byzantines, it was an important religious centre but the trade routes had once again shifted and it was not until the time of Saladin, in the 12th century, that the city enjoyed a brief rebirth before shrinking again to an obscure village that was 'rediscovered' by British travellers in 1751.

EAST MEETS WEST

Palmyra was a strikingly mixed city. It had a Greek constitution, Seleucid dating, Macedonian calendar, Semitic alphabet and Aramaic as its everyday language, although Greek and Latin were also in use.

This mixed heritage was reflected in the physical fabric of the city. Colonnaded streets, baths, a theatre and an agora reflect the Greco–Roman influence, as do the Classical Greek floor plans of the merchants' mansions excavated by archaeologists, complete with beautiful mosaics. The city's main temple, dedicated to the Babylonian god Bel, featured Greek columns around the *cella* (the inner chamber) and imitative Graeco–Roman pediments, but the overall layout of the *temenos*, or sacred district, was based on Semitic models (like the Temple of Solomon).

Visitors today can still see many remains. The theatre has been partially restored and is probably the highlight, with a grand backdrop to the main stage, designed to resemble the façade of a palace. Many columns still stand along the main colonnaded street, with richly decorated monumental archways and the remains of the Temple of Neb (the Babylonian god of writing and wisdom). The street leads towards the Diocletian Baths (built between 293 and 303CE, when the city was mainly a garrison town), notable for four pink sandstone columns probably brought all the way from Egypt. It may originally have been intended as a palace, but was requisitioned for its new role when the military moved in.

ⓘ information

Location

Palmyra
Province of Homs
Syria

 **UNESCO site**
whc.unesco.org/en/list/23

Transport

✈ Lattakia

PETRA

See map p.7 ⑥

LOCATION:	SOUTHERN JORDAN
CONSTRUCTED:	*c.*2ND CENTURY BCE
ABANDONED:	*c.*6TH CENTURY CE
BUILT BY:	NABATAEANS
KEY FEATURES:	SIQ GORGE; ROCK-HEWN BUILDINGS; URN TOMBS; TREASURY; AMPHITHEATRE; BYZANTINE CHURCH AND MOSAICS

Petra is a unique and beautiful ancient city with biblical roots that grew to become one of the greatest trading centres in the world.

Visitors approaching Petra by the Siq (Arabic for the 'shaft'), a winding gorge over 1.6 kilometres (1 mile) long come face to face with a building known as Al-Khazneh (the Treasury), which is 40 metres (131 feet) high, with great pillars, pediments, porticoes and statues, carved directly into the cliff face. From here the gorge continues north-eastwards past more façades, bends north at a great Roman-style amphitheatre and eventually opens out onto a broad valley studded with ruins and dotted with yet more enormous tombs carved into the rock. These are the remains of Petra, the Greek name for the city, which means, simply, 'The Rock'.

AN OASIS CITY

Petra was the capital of the ancient Nabataean civilization, which flowered into a Golden Age around the 2nd and 1st centuries BCE, but with roots much further back in time. In its prime, it was the junction of the world's main trade routes linking East to West, a clearing house for caravans bringing silks and other goods from China via the Silk Road to be exchanged for the produce of Rome and the Mediterranean. Clever hydrological engineering and husbandry of resources allowed the Nabataeans to create an artificial oasis at Petra, so that a great city, renowned from Carthage to China, could flourish in the midst of a barren desert region.

◀ **Al-Khazneh.** The Treasury – a rock-hewn tomb that confronts visitors approaching via the gorge. According to legend, treasure is concealed within the giant urn above the entrance.

The region has been occupied since the Stone Age and it is likely that the dramatic setting and geology of the place, with its unfailing springs and narrow canyons gouged into the base of an imposing mountain (Jabal Haroun, or Aaron's Mount, said to be the resting place of Aaron, brother of Moses), made it both religiously and militarily significant from prehistoric times onwards. Deposits of copper ore also made it a centre of early metallurgy with the dawn of the Bronze Age.

THE WEALTH OF NATIONS

The Bronze Age witnessed the rise of 'superpowers', such as Egypt and Sumer, and a corresponding development of trade. Petra was situated at a crucial juncture of trade routes between Egypt, the Levant and Mesopotamia. The long valley that ran from the Sea of Galilee to the Dead Sea (the Jordan Valley) and then on down to the Gulf of Aqaba and the Red Sea (the Wadi Arabah), formed a natural highway for trade from what would later become the port of Ezion–Geber (now Aqaba) all the way up to Damascus, Palmyra and the Phoenician ports – this route came to be known as the King's Highway. Petra was right next to the Wadi Arabah.

Meanwhile the route from the Euphrates–Tigris delta across the Arabian deserts to Egypt and the Levant also passed

THE MOST CURSED CITY

The archaeological evidence suggests that Petra did not exist in early biblical times; however, the Bible tells a much different story, in which the fractious relationship between the Edomites of Petra and the ancient Hebrews led the prophets of Israel to call down a battery of curses on the Petrans, making it the most cursed place in the Bible. The lawgiver Moses was the first to curse Petra, but the vitriol really began to flow when the Petrans gloated over the 1st millennium BCE Assyrian and Babylonian conquests of Israel and the subsequent travails of the Hebrews. Isaiah, Jeremiah and Ezekiel all invoked curses of desolation and waste on Petra, too.

through Petra, where it split into the road across the Sinai to Luxor and later Alexandria, and across the Negev to Gaza, gateway to the Mediterranean. Yet another major trade route led up from Aden at the tip of the Arabian Peninsula, along the eastern shore of the Red Sea, to Petra. Maritime trade was still extremely limited by primitive naval technology, so the land routes were pre-eminent. Later they would become even more important, as this Mesopotamian–Mediterranean trade network was plugged into the continent-spanning Silk Road, which disgorged the

▲ **The Monastery.** The largest façade in Petra, measuring 50 metres (164 feet) across and 45 metres (148 feet) high.

wealth of the Orient by sea to ports such as Basra (at the mouth of the Euphrates–Tigris), Aden and Ezion–Geber, and via the land routes further north.

At first Petra proved a handy stronghold for the desert tribes who would raid these rich caravans. Later these tribes would extract tribute for allowing safe passage and offering protection from other raiders. Still later, they would develop into a trading hub, offering supplies, in return making money from taxes and tariffs, and eventually becoming merchants.

As trade increased, so did the strategic and economic importance of Petra, and regional powers vied for control. For instance, Egyptian documents of the early 12th century BCE record pharaonic triumphs over the people of Seir, which was probably a reference to Petra, and by this time the region had been under the hegemony of the Egyptians for many centuries. The earliest recorded kings of Petra date to the 8th century BCE, although several biblical figures, such as Rekem and Balaam, mentioned in Genesis and

▲ **Cave tombs.** Despite an official ban, some of the tombs are still used as homes by local Bedouin.

probably dating to around 1300BCE, may have filled this role. The establishment of the kingdom of Israel, *c.*1000BCE, saw a period of constant warfare between the Hebrews and their Semitic neighbours, including the Petrans, leading the latter to cheer the subjugation of Israel by the Babylonians under Nebuchadnezzar in 586BCE. They thus earned themselves the undying enmity of the Hebrews, as expressed through a range of colourful and vitriolic curses called down by various Old Testament prophets (see box on page 48).

THE NABATAEANS

Around the 6th century BCE, the Edomites who inhabited Petra were displaced by the Nabataeans, a nomadic tribe from northern Arabia. Egyptian and Persian power in the region had given way to Alexander the Great in the 4th century BCE, and his successors, the Ptolemies and Antigonids, battled for control of Petra for 200 years. Eventually, however, both these empires declined and in the power vacuum the Nabataeans flourished. Careful hydrological engineering, including the excavation of a great cistern to capture the flash floods that inundated the dry valley, allowed them to sustain large-scale agriculture and provide valuable resources for the trans-desert caravans. Combined with their control of the trade routes, the Nabataeans grew rich and powerful, minting coins and developing a script that would later become Arabic, now used across much of the Muslim world.

As they became settled and wealthy the Nabataeans began to build free-standing monumental architecture and to excavate magnificent tombs from the sandstone cliffs and mountainsides, with the primary building boom, including construction of the most famous rock-cut tombs, taking place around the end of the 1st century BCE. At first their style was mainly borrowed from the Ptolemaic Egyptians, and later Greek influences took root. Idiosyncratic Nabataean touches include the prevalence of urns atop the rock-cut tomb facades. Many of the buildings would have had lush gardens, while the gorge and valley floors would have been crowded with less permanent wooden structures.

LATER HISTORY OF PETRA

The rise of Rome saw Petra fall into the Roman sphere of influence. Petran princes served with Roman armies and may have belonged to the Roman jet set. Roman custom often saw client kings cede their states to Rome on their demise and in 106CE, with the death of the last Nabataean king, Rabbel II, Petra passed into Roman control. Although the city survived as the capital of Arabia Petraea, the most prosperous of all Roman provinces (at one time it produced a quarter of the economic output of the entire empire), the seeds of Petra's decline had already been sown.

Under the Byzantine Empire (from the 4th century CE), Petra became a centre of Christianity, with a Byzantine church, the incredible mosaic floors of which can still be seen. By the time of the Islamic conquest, Petra was a largely deserted city, damaged by severe earthquakes and without a raison d'être.

Today Petra is probably the biggest tourist attraction in Jordan and continues to be the subject of intensive archaeological study.

ⓘ information

Location
Petra
Jordan

 Archaeological Park site
www.petrapark.com

Transport
 Amman

PERSEPOLIS

See map p.7 ⑦

LOCATION:	FARS PROVINCE, IRAN
CONSTRUCTED:	513BCE
ABANDONED:	c.8TH CENTURY CE
BUILT BY:	DARIUS THE GREAT OF THE ACHAEMENID PERSIAN EMPIRE
KEY FEATURES:	TERRACE; APADANA; HALL OF ONE HUNDRED COLUMNS; TOMBS OF THE KINGS; TREASURY

In the rocky uplands of modern-day Iran, ruins atop a huge terrace bear witness to the glory of a long-vanished kingdom – the Achaemenid Empire, sometimes described as the first world empire.

The ruins of Persepolis lie around 70 kilometres (43½ miles) to the north-east of the city of Shiraz, on the eastern edge of the Marv Dasht plain, in the province of Fars. It was constructed to serve as the ceremonial capital of the Achaemenid Empire.

The Achaemenids were a dynasty of Persian kings who emerged from relative obscurity in the middle of the 6th century BCE when Cyrus II (r. 559–530BCE) unified the competing kingdoms of Persia and swept across the Middle and Near East to acquire a vast empire, snatching the imperial mantle from its ancient Mesopotamian heartland and conquering territories from the Levant to Bactria and Sogdiana in Central Asia. His

heirs extended the empire to Egypt, Asia Minor and into Greece, creating a globe-spanning polity that was the first to connect the Mediterranean world to the borders of India and China in a single kingdom.

NEW EMPEROR, NEW CAPITAL

Cyrus made his capital at Pasargadae, but after the death of his successor Cambyses (522BCE) there was an intense struggle for the throne that ended when Darius I (r. 521–486BCE) assumed the crown. To bolster the legitimacy of his claim he founded a new and glorious capital on a site chosen for its impressive aspect, where an imposing terrace of stone would support great buildings calculated to awe subjects and visiting rulers alike.

Sculptures. Huge sculptures of bulls and hybrid ▶ beasts flank the doors of Xerxes's gatehouse.

▲ **The Great Staircase.** Magnificent bas reliefs adorn the staircase leading up to the terrace.

TERRACE AND MAIN BUILDINGS

The terrace was 450 metres (1,476 feet) long and 300 metres (984 feet) wide – covering over 125,000 square metres (1⅓ million square feet), and rose 14 metres (46 feet) above the plain. Imposing staircases from the plain led up to the terrace, with steps wide and low enough for horses to pass freely up and down.

The main staircase onto the site was on the north-west corner, leading to a huge gatehouse built by Xerxes, the ruins of which still remain. Massive double doors of wood bound in metal gave on to a hall with four 12-metre (39¼-feet) high columns. Two other doorways led out to the eastern and southern sectors of the site. The doors were flanked by carved bulls and hybrid beasts – winged, human-headed bulls – a motif of kingship borrowed from Mesopotamia.

To the south of the gate stood the greatest building, the Apadana, an audience hall begun by Darius and completed by Xerxes. The main hall was 60 metres (197 feet) on each side, with high columns holding up a roof of oak and cedar beams, imported from the Levant. The capitals of each column were carved into the shapes of animal heads. Along three sides were deep porticoes with more great columns, and huge staircases led up to the north and east façades. These still stand, and are decorated with impressive reliefs, which are among the finest surviving examples of Achaemenid art. They show 23 pairs of delegates from the nations of the empire, bringing tribute for the king. Some of them hold barsom sheaves – bundles of sticks/grasses that had a sacred, ceremonial purpose – and it is thought that the relief may show the celebration of the Persian New Year festival. It is interesting to note that depictions of the king at Persepolis appear to show him as much larger than his subjects, reflecting the ultimate purpose of the decoration and indeed the overall architecture of the city.

On the eastern side of the terrace sit the remains of another audience hall, known as the Hall of One Hundred Columns. Behind it lies a lesser building, known as the Treasury, where archaeologists recovered a cache of clay tablets that proved to be records kept by financial officers (more were found in the city walls).

Side by side behind the Apadana are two magnificent palaces. On the western side sit the remains of the palace of Darius, with suites of rooms running alongside a pillared hall. Ornate carvings show the hero king struggling with real and mythical animals. To the east of this lie the remains of Xerxes's even larger palace, and alongside it is a long building traditionally known as Xerxes's Harem, although there is no proof that this is what it was.

POMP AND CEREMONY

The evidence of the site shows that Persepolis was more of a ceremonial and symbolic capital than a genuine centre of government. To begin with, it was not geographically favourably situated in terms of the vast Persian Empire. Cities such as Babylon and Susa were closer to the main centres of population, economic activity and transport links. Persepolis was comparatively remote and inaccessible, reflected by the fact that the city was relatively unknown to the ancient Greeks until Alexander invaded the Persian Empire. The site itself shows that it was not well suited to be a major centre of population. Plumbing and sewage supply was relatively limited and there is more evidence of people living on the plain around the terrace than on the terrace itself.

It seems likely that one of the main roles of Persepolis was, on the rare occasions that the court was in residence, to function as a kind of theatre, where elaborate ceremonies drove home the magnificence and power of the king, thus asserting the legitimacy of his rule and impressing visiting dignitaries.

When the court was absent, it is likely that few people actually lived on the terrace. The Treasury records indicate that around 1,300 workmen tended to the site as a sort of skeleton staff, and these men and their families probably lived in cruder structures just beyond the walls of the city.

TOMBS OF THE KINGS

Among the ceremonial functions of the city were probably those involved in the funerals of dead kings. Carved into the rocks behind the city are an unfinished tomb and two completed ones, which probably belonged to Artaxerxes II and III, late kings of the dynasty, while a few kilometres to the north of Persepolis is a more significant site where the tombs of four kings are cut into a cliff, carved into magnificent façades. The site is called Naqsh-e Rustam – 'the picture of Rustam'. Rustam or Rostam was a Persian folk hero during the Middle Ages, by which time knowledge of the ancient Achaemenids had been largely lost, and it seems that the local people mistook the elaborate carvings for depictions of their legendary hero. In fact

▼ **Capitals.** The columns at Persepolis were topped with elaborate capitals, such as this double-headed griffin.

the tombs belong to Darius the Great, Xerxes and their successors. They would once have been filled with stupendous treasures but they were looted (probably in ancient times) and now stand empty.

THE OXUS TREASURE

It is possible, however, to get a flavour of the grave goods that might have been interred in the tombs from the Oxus Treasure, the finest surviving collection of Achaemenid artefacts. The treasure came to light in the late 19th century, when it was dug out of a hill beside the Oxus River in Central Asia, sold to merchants, stolen by bandits and then recovered by a British political officer. Eventually most of it ended up in the British Museum, London. Current thinking is that the hoard of gold and silver ornaments, figurines, jewellery, votive pieces and coins was buried to protect it from raiders, but had initially resided in a temple in Bactria, on the edge of the Achaemenid Empire, and that it was at least partly made up of pieces looted from tombs. Many of the pieces show designs similar or practically identical to reliefs at Persepolis, and it is plausible to suggest that before they were buried as grave goods or carried to Bactria, they graced the bodies and costumes of visitors to the court.

ALEXANDER'S REVENGE

In 333BCE Alexander the Great invaded the Persian Empire and three years later he was at the gates of Persepolis. According to the ancient accounts the Macedonian king was astounded at the great wealth of the city, and he was said to have employed a baggage train of 20,000 mules and 3,000 camels to cart it away. Having looted Persepolis and occupied it for around three months, Alexander destroyed it, probably for strategic reasons (it would have been dangerous to leave a fortified city behind him). Under his successors and the Second Persian Empire of the Sassanids, the locale retained its status as regional capital but probably only ever regained a fraction of its former glories, and after the Islamic conquest the city declined still further until it was completely abandoned.

---

 information

Location
Persepolis
Central Iran

 UNESCO site
whc.unesco.org/en/list/114

Transport
 Shiraz

BABYLON

See map p.7 (8)

LOCATION: EUPHRATES RIVER, SOUTH OF BAGHDAD, IRAQ

CONSTRUCTED: BEFORE 2400BCE

ABANDONED: c.1ST CENTURY CE

BUILT BY: BABYLONIANS

KEY FEATURES: CITY WALLS; ISHTAR GATE; ETEMENANKI ZIGGURAT; ESAGIL TEMPLE; HANGING GARDENS

A city of such greatness and magnificence that its name and repute have far outlived its physical fabric, Babylon was a place of magic and learning, exile and sadness, power and glory, which has left an indelible mark on global culture even as it crumbles into dust at an accelerating rate.

Situated on the banks of the Euphrates about 80 kilometres (50 miles) south of modern Baghdad, Babylon was a great city for nearly two millennia, yet was effectively abandoned by the start of the Common Era.

CITY OF THE LAW-GIVER

Babylon first rose to prominence and power under the Babylonian king Hammurabi, who ruled from 1792–1750BCE, establishing what is now known as the Old Babylonian kingdom. At that time, Babylon was probably the largest city in the world. Temples, shrines and public buildings multiplied and the city acquired imposing walls. Hammurabi is best known today for his code, among the oldest set of laws known to mankind, which were inscribed on large stelae written in Akkadian, the day-to-day language of the Babylonians at this time, and displayed in public for all to see.

The Old Babylonian kingdom was short lived and was soon conquered by first the Hittites and then the Kassites. However, the city itself remained the regional capital for several centuries until suffering declining fortunes during the early 1st millennium BCE, with climate fluctuations, famine, plague and the depredations of nomadic raiders

◀ **The Fall of Babylon.** This 19th-century engraving by French artist Gustave Doré is an impression of the fall of Babylon to the Achaemenid Persians in 539BCE.

taking their toll. Meanwhile, the Assyrians to the north grew in power until Babylon fell under their sway around 800BCE.

The Assyrians renewed and enlarged the city, but they struggled constantly to suppress the rebellious Babylonians. In 689BCE the Assyrian king, Sennacherib, sacked the city and had it razed to the ground, but just a few decades later the Assyrian Empire collapsed and King Nabopolassar established a Neo-Babylonian dynasty that reached its apogee under his son, Nebuchadnezzar (r. 604–562BCE).

NEBUCHADNEZZAR AND THE HANGING GARDENS

Under Nebuchadnezzar, the city reached its greatest magnificence, as its population climbed above the 200,000 mark – the first city in human history to do so. He enlarged the empire as far as the shores of the Mediterranean and engaged in an extensive series of works, enlarging the city and building vast palaces. For his wife, homesick for the lush vegetation of her homeland, he reputedly built a series of hanging gardens that sat atop a great hall and were watered by a ceaseless cascade mechanically extracted from the river.

This Neo-Babylonian Empire was also short lived, falling to the Achaemenid Persians under Cyrus in 539BCE, until it was conquered by Alexander the Great in 331BCE. Alexander renovated parts of the city, added buildings, including a theatre, and encouraged commerce, arts and the sciences, but his death not long after spelt doom for Babylon. The fragile empire he had so quickly forged fell apart just as rapidly, as his generals fought for control of the different regions. As the effective capital of the world, Babylon found itself at the centre of a series of wars that steadily depleted its material and human resources. Mass deportations, such as one recorded in a tablet of 275BCE, further diminished the failing city's population and the city finally died with a whimper at some point during the hegemony of the Parthian Empire, which ruled Mesopotamia until the 3rd century CE.

REDISCOVERING BABYLON

When European travellers once again began to frequent the region, all that remained were a number of tells – mounds built up as generations occupied the same site for millennia. Armed with copies of Herodotus and other ancient writers, gentlemen adventurers sought to relate the barren mounds to the Classical accounts, but not until the methodical excavations of the Deutsche–Orient Gesellschaft (German–Orient Society), led by Dr Robert Koldewey and carried out from 1899–1917, was the ancient city properly rediscovered. The city that Koldewey's team painstakingly

▲ **Hanging Gardens.** These reconstructed ruins are speculated to be the remains of the famous gardens.

uncovered was essentially Nebuchadnezzar's Babylon. They traced its walls, palaces and temples, and even identified the possible inspirations for the legendary Tower of Babel and Hanging Gardens.

ROUGH GUIDE TO BABYLON

Ancient Babylon was roughly rectangular in shape, oriented on a south-west–north-east angle, split in two by the Euphrates about a third of the way in from the west. The most significant locations were on the eastern side. A huge wall ran around the entire city. Herodotus famously claimed that it was so wide that there was room enough on top for 'a four-horse chariot to run'. In fact Koldewey discovered that it was 30 metres (98½ feet) wide – enough room for two chariots to pass. The wall was studded with great towers at regular intervals and stretched for 18 kilometres (11¼ miles), while the city covered an area of 8.5 square kilometres (3¼ square miles), making it the largest of the ancient Mesopotamian cities.

Perhaps the most impressive find was the Ishtar Gate, a ceremonial entrance to the city created by Nebuchadnezzar to strike awe into the hearts of visitors. They were presented with a high arch spanning the gap between two mighty 25-metre (82-feet) high towers decorated with brightly coloured glazed tiles and reliefs of fearsome dragons, lions and bulls, all raised on a platform 15 metres (49¼ feet) above ground level. The gate now resides in Berlin's Pergamon Museum. Leading from the Ishtar Gate into the heart of the city, Koldewey traced the course of a processional way 20 metres (65½ feet) wide, also lined with glazed tiles and reliefs of lions. This formed the main axis of the city, and ran parallel to the river, past palaces and temples, until reaching a street that ran off to the left, towards the river, and which passed between the two central structures of Babylon – the Etemenanki and the Esagil.

▼ **Ishtar Gate.** A fierce lion made from glazed tiles patrols the Ishtar Gate.

THE AXIS MUNDI

The Etemenanki (meaning 'the house that is the foundation of heaven and Earth') was a ziggurat, or stepped tower, which represented – in a very literal fashion for the Babylonians – the *axis mundi* or axis of the world. The Etemenanki ziggurat may well have been the basis for the legend of the Tower of Babel. At its base, it was 91 metres (295 feet) square, with a broad staircase ascending its seven stages, but it cannot be said for sure how tall it was.

The Esagil was the temple of Marduk, the tutelary deity of Babylon and the leader of the Babylonian pantheon. Here dwelt the idol of Marduk – a golden statue – together with the idols of deities from other city states within Babylon's sphere of influence.

Koldewey also discovered the throne room of Nebuchadnezzar, a 50-metre (164-feet) long room magnificently decorated with coloured glazed bricks and reliefs showing lions and trees of life, and a series of underground chambers with barrel-vaulted roofs, asphalt waterproofing and a system of wells. Koldewey was convinced that 'a mechanic hydraulic machine stood there, which worked on the same principle as our chain pump', and that he had discovered the site of the Hanging Gardens of Babylon. Modern archaeological opinion is divided, however, and the city of Nineveh is said by some to be a more likely location for the legendary gardens, if they existed at all.

MODERN BABYLON

More recently Babylon has become a figurative and literal battleground in the Gulf conflicts. Following on from Nebuchadnezzar, who had the millions of bricks used stamped with his name and a proclamation of his glory, Saddam Hussein attempted something similar. In 1985, he started reconstructing the city with bricks stamped 'This was built by Saddam Hussein, son of Nebuchadnezzar, to glorify Iraq'. More recently, US forces have occupied the area and their helicopters, trucks, earthmovers and troops have been blamed for significant damage to the ruins.

 information

Location

Babylon

Southern Iraq

 Iraqi Government site

www.culture-iraq.com/
pages/babylon-ruins.html

Transport

 Baghdad

EUROPE

From Bronze Age Knossos to doomed Pompeii, the cities in this chapter span 1,500 years of history, yet there is a clear connection and sense of continuity running through their four stories, which chart the development of the Classical world in Europe from its earliest times to the threshold of its greatest empire: the Roman Empire. Until the late 19th century it had been believed that European civilization started with the ancient Greeks in around 800BCE, but Schliemann's excavations at Mycenae appeared to push this date back to at least 1500BCE. Schliemann's discoveries inspired the excavation of Knossos, which revealed an even older civilization – the Minoans: the first European civilization.

A cultural thread runs from this early European civilization at Knossos through the Mycenaeans to the Greeks and eventually from them to the Romans, and this thread links all four cities in this chapter. Akrotiri, on modern-day Santorini (but originally on a much larger island that was largely destroyed when the volcano of Thera erupted in a colossal explosion c.1625BCE), was a town of the Cycladic culture with close ties to the dominant Minoan culture on Crete, but which also traded with Mycenae on mainland Greece. Entremont, in southern France (then Gaul), was a settlement on the fringes of the Greco–Roman world, built by Celto–Ligurians, but inspired by and modelled on nearby Greek colonies, and later closely involved with the expanding empire of Rome. Pompeii was a thriving city of late Republican Rome (although originally Latin rather than Roman) and at one time may well have been the base for merchants and artisans who traded with Entremont. Through the stories of these four cities, we can follow the development and spread of European civilization.

Akrotiri fresco. A detail of one of the most famous frescoes in Akrotiri, from the West ▶
House, which is believed to have belonged to a naval commander. It shows two boys
returning from a fishing expedition, laden with the fish they have caught.

ENTREMONT

See map p.7 (9)

LOCATION:	PROVENCE, FRANCE
CONSTRUCTED:	c.180BCE
ABANDONED:	c.90BCE
BUILT BY:	SALYENS
KEY FEATURES:	OLD AND NEW TOWN; CITY WALL; HYPOSTYLE HALL; RELIEFS AND IDOLS OF HEADS AND HEROES; OLIVE PRESSES

Traditionally Western European history before the coming of the Romans has been seen as a dark age of savage tribes and primitive villages of rude wattle and daub huts, but a large and sophisticated Gallic settlement in southern France shows that this picture is misconceived.

Entremont is a 2nd- to 1st-century BCE settlement of the Celto–Ligurian Salyens (known as the Saluvii by ancient Greco–Roman writers) in Provence in southern France. Here, on the fringes of the Greco–Latin world, a large town of regular gridlike streets, well-planned fortifications, multiple-storey grand public buildings and elaborate religious precincts flourished, until besieged and sacked by a Roman army.

◀ **Town plan.** The lower courses of walls were constructed of stone and have survived to preserve the plan and layout of much of the town.

GREEKS AND GAULS

Around 600BCE, Greeks from Phocea founded a colony called Massalia (modern Marseilles) near the mouth of the Rhône, a great river that provided access to much of France and central Western Europe. All the valuable natural wealth of Europe, from amber and furs to tin and slaves, was available to the Greeks. In return, they traded the products of the Mediterranean – wine, fish products, glass, worked metals, and, above all, quality pottery.

The Greek colony had a significant impact on societies reaching far up into Europe, but especially on those along the Rhône and the Cote d'Azur, the trading routes to and from southern France. And because Greek and Latin writers recorded some of the interactions between the colonists and their neighbours, we know the names of many of these groups. One

▲ **Limestone heads.** Groups of these sculptures of severed heads were found at the sanctuary at Entremont. They date to the 2nd century BCE.

that particularly stands out was the Salyens, a confederation of tribes of Celts and Ligurians, the indigenous peoples of the area.

The Salyens had a fraught relationship with the Greek colony. Although there was considerable trade and peaceful contact, there was also occasional outbreaks of violence. In the 4th and 3rd centuries BCE, to protect their trade routes against piracy, the Greeks founded subsidiary colonies along the coast such as Nikaia (Nice) and Antipolis (Antibes), but these too came under threat from land-based forces. The Salyens gained a reputation for extreme barbarity, particularly owing to their typically Celtic custom of taking heads as trophies.

SETTLEMENT AT ENTREMONT

The site at Entremont probably had religious or ritual significance before it was settled, as indicated by *stelae* (carved stone posts) from around 500BCE, that were reused in later buildings, but the first settlement on the site dates back to around 180BCE. It was small, only about 1 hectare (2½ acres) in area, and was situated at the summit of a plateau. The edges of the settlement were aligned with the south and west sides of the plateau and it had the shape of a displaced square (i.e. a parallelogram). The northern side of the town, which gave on to the open plateau, was fortified with a 1.36-metre (4½-feet) wide wall that had three towers. Within this wall, 3-metre (10-feet) wide streets were laid out in a regular criss-cross pattern. The streets were not paved, although they were set with stones and fragments of pottery to help stabilize them.

Blocks of houses were subdivided by walls of stone blocks with mud bricks for their upper courses. Roofs were made of wood frames and wattle and daub. Mud bricks were used to create small structures inside the houses, such as hearths, but fireplaces were also often built in the street outside the house because of the limited space.

One of the blocks was probably devoted to crafts such as metal working, but on the whole the evidence is that the inhabitants of lived at a near-subsistence level.

THE NEW TOWN

Around 150BCE, the town was dramatically enlarged and seems to have taken a step up economically, but there is also evidence of a major shift in the social structure. The new town was much bigger – an area of about 3.5 hectares (8¾ acres) – and had an extensive defensive wall that was 3.5 metres (11½ feet) thick and up to 7 metres (23 feet) high.

The new town was also organized into slightly off-square blocks, but these were more than twice as large as those in the old town. Most of the streets were wider and the houses were larger. There is evidence that more activities were going on in the domestic spaces. In particular, many counterweights for presses have been found. Chemical analysis of residues from jars and the floors of houses indicate that these presses were for producing olive oil, so it looks as though the people of Entremont had developed a significant cottage industry.

The biggest building of the new town backed onto the line of the old town wall, which had been destroyed and recycled. It was a monumental hypostyle hall, 20 metres (65½ feet) long and 5 metres (16½ feet) wide, with a series of wooden pillars supporting a second storey. The walls were made of stone in the lower courses and packed clay in the upper, with a timber-framed façade. The pillars of the façade rested upon a long stone bar, or *stylobate*, which included stones previously used in the primitive sanctuary that predated the settlement. Twenty skulls pierced with holes have been found scattered around the *stylobate*, suggesting that the façade was decorated with heads nailed to the timbers. The floor of the building was fine-packed clay, while the internal walls were coated with white lime. The street in front of the hall was enlarged and the effect was to create an impressive public building set apart from the rest of the town. Although admittedly probably based on Greek models, which the Salyens would have seen in Massalia or other colonies, this building is a remarkable symbol of Gallic sophistication and ability.

THE CULT OF THE HEROES

Arguably the most important parts of the settlement were the four religious sanctuaries. These are marked by carved *stelae* and lintels, sculptures, statues and skulls. Some of the lintels have recesses for heads or skulls, alongside reliefs of heads. The sculptures show heroic figures, seated in Buddhalike poses, with weapons and trophies, including skulls. The heads and skulls might represent either trophies of the dead or relics of revered ancestors.

Although Celtic society is traditionally renowned as an egalitarian one, the evidence of this and other sites is that it was becoming much more stratified, with aristocratic lineages asserting their superiority and dominant status. In the Entremont sanctuaries, the heroes are displayed in close association with representations of these aristocratic lineages, suggesting that the ruling classes were trying to appropriate the pre-existing cult of the hero to bolster their own prestige and status.

THE END OF ENTREMONT

In 125BCE, Roman forces moved against the Salyens, but Entremont, probably the Salyen capital, resisted the legions. In 123BCE, under the Roman consul C. Sextius Calvinus, another force besieged the city, and this time the Roman military might was too much and the city was taken and sacked. According to ancient sources the Saluvian king and his nobles fled to the north and took refuge with a tribe called the Allobriges, while the surviving inhabitants of Entremont were deported (possibly into slavery), with the exception of a nobleman called Craton, a Roman collaborator. Along with 900 of his people he was allowed to remain at Entremont, where they apparently lived until *c.*90BCE, when a second military destruction suggests that Craton's descendants did not maintain their cordial relations with the Romans. After this the site was abandoned.

▲ **Furnaces.** These structures would have been used for metal production, which is one of the more sophisticated activities carried out in the original settlement.

(i) information

Location

Entremont

Aix-en-Provence

France

 Archaeological site

www.entremont.culture.
gouv.fr

Transport

✈ Marseille

 Aix-en-Provence

POMPEII

See map p.7 (10)

LOCATION: BAY OF NAPLES, ITALY

CONSTRUCTED: 6TH CENTURY BCE

ABANDONED: 79CE

BUILT BY: ETRUSCANS? ROMANS

KEY FEATURES: PRESERVED STREETS AND BUILDINGS; THERMOPOLIA; BROTHEL; GRAFFITI; MOSAICS AND MURALS

Arguably the most important archaeological site in the world, Pompeii is also one of the largest, in terms of coherent, contiguous ruins. But for recent closures to help conserve the fragile site, a modern visitor would be able to explore almost exactly the same geography as his ancient counterpart – an entire city, from the grandest public buildings to the meanest back-alley hovel, preserved to an unprecedented extent by fallout from the eruption of Vesuvius in 79CE.

Pompeii is a ruined town on the lower slopes of Mount Vesuvius on the Bay of Naples. In its heyday as many as 20,000 people lived here and the town was prosperous thanks to the rich, fertile volcanic soils of the region, local industry, maritime trade coming into Italy via the nearby ports (in ancient times it was much closer to the sea than it is now) and the popularity of the Bay of Naples area as a fashionable resort and leisure destination for Roman senators, noblemen and businessmen.

The oldest settlement on the site dates back to the Iron Age, in the 8th century BCE, although nearby sites date back as far as the Bronze Age, and suffered a similar fate to Pompeii itself – caught unawares by the previous eruption of Vesuvius, some 1,800 years earlier. Pompeii itself was founded in the 6th century BCE, either by a local tribe, the Oscans, or possibly by Greek colonists or the Etruscans. By the 4th century BCE, the area had fallen under the hegemony of Rome, but Pompeii did not become a Roman town until it joined with other towns in the region in an unsuccessful rebellion against Rome, found itself on the

◀ **Courtyard.** This ruined villa at Pompeii is set around a courtyard in typical Roman style.

▲ **Temple of Jupiter.** One of the primary public buildings in the forum, with Mount Vesuvius in the background.

losing side and was finally declared a Roman colony in 80BCE. Many of the buildings visible at Pompeii today, including much of the infrastructure, were built in the Roman period. The reign of Augustus (30BCE–14CE) saw particularly intensive building work.

ROUGH GUIDE TO POMPEII

Excavations have uncovered 44 of the 66 hectares (109 of the 163 acres) occupied by the city. It is roughly oval in shape, with the long axis oriented east–west. A city wall, pierced by seven main gates, encloses

the whole. Most visits begin at the Marine Gate in the south-west, which leads almost immediately to the forum, the centre of public life in Pompeii and the site of a bustling market. Around the forum are many of the main public buildings, including the Temples of Apollo and Jupiter, the basilica (where legal business was conducted), one of the city's baths, the *macellum* (market / shopping mall) and the local government offices.

South-east of these is Pompeii's 'leisure complex', a group of buildings including the

Samnite Palaestra (a kind of gym), the theatre and the *odeon*, the gladiator's barracks and the Temple of Isis. Although an eastern cult, worship of Isis became extremely popular and this temple was the only one to be fully restored after the earthquake of 62CE (see page 76).

(see page 76)

Running east from the forum, passing to the north of the leisure zone, is the Via dell'Abbondanza, a long, mostly straight road that runs all the way to the Sarno Gate at the eastern end of the city. Along or just off it can be seen many of the most interesting private or commercial buildings of Pompeii, including a fullery, the brothel, the Stabian Baths and the Thermopolium of Vetutius Placidus. A *thermopolium* was a kind of café, which served hot food to customers who stood at a bar into which were sunk terracotta containers for hot stews, soups, etc. Pompeii's *thermopolia* seem to have done a roaring trade, indicated by the bag of over 1,000 coins discovered at one such establishment, believed to be the takings on the day that the eruption struck. The Via dell'Abbondanza leads towards the *palaestra* (exercise courts for wrestling/ boxing – a kind of Roman gym) and the amphitheatre. With seating for 20,000 people, this is the oldest stone amphitheatre in the world. Gladiatorial games were staged here, but it was closed down for a decade from 59CE after spectators from Pompeii

and the nearby town of Nuceria started a riot. North of the Via dell'Abbondanza are the main parts of the city that have yet to be excavated.

In the north-west section of Pompeii are some of the most interesting and important private houses. For instance, the House of the Vettii is one of the most famous in Pompeii. The owners are thought to have been the Vettii brothers, whose signet rings were discovered on the site. They may have been wine merchants and used their riches to create a beautiful and stylish house that would show off their wealth and taste. In particular, they created a large garden that can be seen from the street through the front door; it was decorated with marble and bronze statues, some of which spouted water into basins. Around the garden is a portico, decorated with elaborate murals.

Diagonally across an intersection from here is the House of the Faun, named for the statue of a 'faun' (actually a satyr) found at the site. The largest private house in Pompeii, it was possibly built in the 2nd century BCE and after the Roman conquest it may well have housed one of the city's new rulers. Its interior was decorated to underscore the wealth of its occupant, with extremely detailed (and therefore enormously expensive) mosaics, including the famous replica of a Greek painting showing Alexander the Great defeating the Persian king Darius at the Battle of Issus, which is made up of over a million *tesserae* (tiny tiles).

Leaving from the city's north-western gate, the Herculaneum Gate, the visitor passes through a cemetery and then reaches the Villa of the Mysteries, which is named after the *megalographia* (lifesize mural) that runs around all four walls of one of the rooms. This unique frieze is believed by many to show various stages of initiation into the rites of the Dionysian Mysteries, one of several religions/personal growth movements that were popular in the ancient world. Only those who were initiated knew the secrets of these Mystery religions and were forbidden to reveal them, so this mural is one of the primary (and only) sources for our knowledge of this important element of Roman life.

THE END OF POMPEII

In 62CE, a severe earthquake struck the Bay of Naples region, badly damaging many buildings in Pompeii and other towns. Today vulcanologists understand that this was probably an omen of the much worse catastrophe to come, signifying an upwelling of magma through the crust beneath the mountain. With nearly two millennia elapsed since the last eruption, the Romans had no idea what a threat the volcano posed, still less that Vesuvius is of the type of volcano that erupts more violently the longer the periods between eruptions.

Although the 62CE earthquake caused alarm and fear, and many left the area altogether, there is clear evidence that extensive rebuilding of Pompeii started immediately. Pompeii was too prosperous for its citizens to abandon.

▲ **Bakery.** The millstones at this bakery are remarkably well preserved. The slots in the sides of the stones were for staves to be inserted so that they could be turned to grind grain.

Around 1pm in the afternoon on 24 August 79CE (this is the traditionally attributed date, but cutting-edge research at the site has led to the controversial suggestion that the eruption actually took place later that year), after days of tremors, plumes of gas and the ominous failure of springs around the mountain's flanks, Vesuvius erupted. The first phase of the eruption was what vulcanologists call Plinian, in which gas-rich, frothy, highly pressurized magma from the top of the magma column blasts high into the atmosphere, carrying with it huge chunks of the mountain. An enormous mushroom cloud of fire, ash, smoke and rubble reached

30 kilometres (18½ miles) into the air and then began to rain down as ash and light pumice, with the occasional heavy chunk of rock. In this phase of the eruption 2.6 cubic kilometres (½ cubic mile) of rock was blasted skywards at a rate of 150,000 tons a second.

For the people living around Vesuvius this must have been a terrifying sight, made even more scary when the cloud blotted out the Sun and the day turned to blackest night. A steady rain of ash and pumice started to weigh down and then collapse roofs, killing many. Others were killed by falling rocks.

But at this stage, although there was panic, there was a relatively low risk of death. Most of the population, generally estimated to be about 12,000 at this point, were able to wade through the ash and light pumice, and flee the town.

The Plinian phase continued for about 18 hours, but around 7pm on the following day the much more lethal Peléan phase began. As the pressure inside the volcano lessened and the heavier, less gassy magma reached the top of the column, the plume of material collapsed to ground level and what

▼ **Venus Marina.** The House of Venus Marina, named after this fresco, is located near the Palaestra in Region II.

had been an airborne cloud turned into a pyroclastic flow – a rolling, ground-hugging avalanche of super-heated gas, smoke and ash, preceded by a shockwave of heat at temperatures up to 800°C (1,472°F). People in its path were either instantly carbonized, or choked and baked within a few seconds. Buried within the layers of ash and loose rock that continued to accrete, their bodies decomposed to leave voids. Ingenious mid-19th century Italian archaeologist Giuseppe Fiorelli would later inject these voids with plaster to create casts, preserving, for our horrid fascination, the forms of people in their death throes, right down to the expressions of terror on their faces.

How many were killed? It is known that virtually the whole population of nearby Herculaneum, which suffered a similar fate, perished in the pyroclastic flow. They had made it as far as the seashore, but tsunamis that accompanied the eruption made it impossible to evacuate by ship and the terrible cloud caught them sheltering in boat sheds and the seafront arcade. But only

around 2,000 bodies have been recovered from Pompeii and the surrounding area, and it is often assumed that most of the inhabitants of Pompeii escaped.

However, contemporary accounts make it clear that for the region as a whole this was a catastrophe of unprecedented scale, suggesting that tens of thousands were lost at minimum. And while it was normal practice to rebuild towns after natural disasters, the Romans never settled at Pompeii again. So perhaps the missing Pompeians did not escape death – it is simply that the fatal cloud overtook them on the roads south from Pompeii and that the huge mass of carbonized bodies lies beneath unexcavated and unexplored countryside.

Pompeii was rediscovered in 1748 and has been progressively excavated ever since. But archaeologists have found evidence that there was extensive salvage and looting of the site in ancient times. As soon as the dust had settled it seems that enterprising Romans returned and dug down to look for valuables. The site is riddled with tunnels.

(i) information

Location

Pompeii
Naples
Italy

 Travel site
www.italylogue.com/featured-articles/visiting-pompeii-in-italy.html

Transport

✈ Naples

 Pompeii Scavi-Villa dei Misteri

AKROTIRI

See map p.7

LOCATION:	SANTORINI, GREECE
CONSTRUCTED:	*c.*2000BCE
ABANDONED:	1625 OR 1545BCE
BUILT BY:	CYCLADIC CULTURE
KEY FEATURES:	FRESCOES; TWO-STOREY HOUSES; LUSTRAL BASINS; ADVANCED PLUMBING; THE WEST HOUSE

Around 1625BCE (or possibly 1545BCE – there is fierce dispute over the exact dating), the volcanic island of Thera, one of the Cyclades islands between mainland Greece and Crete, exploded in an eruption that measured 7 on the Volcanic Explosivity Index. The tsunamis generated by the eruption would have been up to 150 metres (492 feet) high according to some estimates. Four times as much material was ejected into the atmosphere as during the famous explosion at Krakatau in 1883 and a blanket of ash and rock up to 50 metres (164 feet) thick settled on the remnants of the island (today the shattered island is an archipelago known as Santorini). Buried beneath this volcanic fallout was the ancient seaport at modern Akrotiri, which lay hidden for three and half millennia until in 1967 renowned Greek archaeologist Spyridon Marinatos began excavations.

What he revealed, and subsequent excavations continue to investigate, was a Cycladic version of Pompeii (see page 76), but with important differences from the Roman town. Whereas the unfortunate Latins were caught unawares and suffered grisly deaths, the inhabitants of Akrotiri seem to have managed to evacuate the town, taking all their portable valuables with them. No uninterred human remains have been found nor have any precious objects, with one exception, an intriguing golden ibex figurine that was hidden beneath a floor – perhaps simply forgotten or perhaps buried for ritual reasons, like figurines found in Neolithic Çatalhöyük (see page 16).

The Delta Complex. This area of Akrotiri includes four ▶ houses, all of which yielded finds such as imported pottery, precious stones and bronze objects.

▲ **Frescos.** The interior of every building in Akrotiri is decorated with frescos and the subjects depicted vary widely.

COSMOPOLITAN HARBOUR TOWN

When the ancient Akrotirians fled they left behind a sophisticated urban development, with spacious multi-storey houses of high-quality masonry equipped with advanced plumbing and sewers, and adorned with vivid and graceful art as fine as any Mediterranean civilization has ever produced. The first settlements on this site date back as far as the Neolithic Era, to before the 4th millennium BCE, but the town reached its height in the Minoan Era (*c*.2000–1500BCE), by which time it had grown into one of the major Bronze Age ports in the eastern Mediterranean. The flourishing palace culture of the Minoans in Crete carried on extensive trade with other Bronze Age superpowers of Egypt, Asia Minor and the Levant, while on the Greek mainland the Mycenaean civilization was gathering strength. Goods and people passed back and forth across the Aegean and Akrotiri was at the centre of this trade – objects have been found here from Crete, Egypt, Anatolia, Cyprus, Syria and the Greek mainland and islands.

The wealth garnered by this trade helped turn Akrotiri into a prosperous town that covered around 20 hectares (49½ acres) and had a population of several thousand. Excavations have shown that although the streets were relatively narrow (probably too narrow for wheeled carts, but wide enough for pack animals), the houses were quite grand. Mostly built of rubble masonry between timber frames, but with some sophisticated dressed-stone block masonry in places (especially on public buildings), many of them were two or even three storeys high. Inside, the lower rooms were probably utilitarian, with kitchen amenities such as mill installations for grinding corn, pestles and mortars and large sunken storage jars. The upper rooms, however, where the owners lived and socialized, were large and airy with big windows. The interiors were plastered and often decorated with the beautiful frescoes that are Akrotiri's most famous legacy.

Some houses had toilets, with wooden benches with openings to clay pipes that connected to the municipal sewers. In some places, twin sets of pipes bringing water into houses suggest that the Akrotirians had hot and cold running water – the former perhaps supplied by hot springs on the volcanic island. Some houses even had separate bathrooms, with walls plastered halfway up to guard against splashing, just like our modern bathrooms. These rooms were painted yellow and may have been equipped with clay bathtubs and bronze vessels for bringing water, such as have been found in one of the settlement's houses. One of the public buildings has a lustral basin – a sunken stone-lined pool probably used for ritual washing. Such sophisticated plumbing is remarkable for an ancient town.

THE END OF AKROTIRI

Marinatos's excavation revealed evidence that Akrotiri had suffered major earthquake damage before it was buried in ash from the eruption of Thera. He theorized that it was this earthquake that had given the inhabitants sufficient warning to evacuate. In practice, the picture is slightly more complex. The careful piling of rubble and the presence of great stone 'demolition' balls probably similar to modern wrecking balls, indicates that after an initial earthquake there was a planned programme of demolition to clear unsafe houses and prepare for reconstruction. It is also clear that this programme of reconstruction was well underway when the evacuation came – and possibly had been for years. Evidently there was sufficient warning – perhaps from

A MINOAN COLONY?

Akrotiri is often described as a Minoan colony or the most famous Minoan site outside Crete. It undoubtedly had strong links with the palace-based culture of the Minoans, as shown by cultural correspondences such as similarities between its frescoes and those found in Crete and by its material culture in terms of pottery and other artefacts. But it is thought likely that it was more representative of the ancient Cycladic culture that had flourished on the Cyclades since c. 3000BCE and that its inhabitants were indigenous, but inevitably influenced by the dominant culture to the south; they probably also absorbed influences from Egypt and other important Bronze Age civilizations.

small tremors or perhaps from an initial, minor eruption and ash fall – that a major eruption was on the way, for this rebuilding was abruptly halted. In the building known as the West House, where plastering and painting was apparently still in progress and was left half finished, abandoned vessels of plaster and paint have been found.

When the eruption came, a deep layer of pumice and ash covered the island so thickly that it was uninhabitable for centuries. Exactly what became of the Akrotirians is impossible to know, but the consequences of the eruption may have been far-reaching. Marinatos was led to begin his excavations at Akrotiri by his theory that the eruption triggered the collapse of Minoan civilization, but in practice the dates do not match up. The palace culture probably survived for another century after Thera exploded, but there is little doubt that the volcano had an impact. While the prevailing winds meant

that most of Crete was not hit by the fallout, the vast tsunami generated by the eruption must have pulverized the Minoan fleet and all the towns along its northern seaboard.

THE FRESCOES

The most striking survivors of the eruption are the many frescoes that decorate the inside of every building in Akrotiri. Only a few of the rooms in each house are decorated and the subjects dealt with vary widely. For instance, in the building known as Xeste 3 (from the Greek *xeste*, meaning 'dressed masonry', such as is seen on this building), which features a lustral basin, the frescoes appear to show parts of a procession or religious ritual. On the upper floor, young women are shown gathering crocuses and bringing them to a central female figure, perhaps a goddess, who is flanked by worshipping animals – a griffin and a monkey. On the ground floor, a fresco on one wall shows a girl carrying a necklace, a girl who has hurt her foot, which is bleeding, and a girl walking in one direction but facing in the other. One wall is dominated by a fresco of a closed door crowned with horns dripping with blood.

By contrast, the private houses show more secular scenes. The building known as the West House, for instance, features a famous fresco of two young fishermen, bearing catches of fish, while another room shows a fleet of ships crossing the sea and putting in at port, while on another wall of the same room two ships disgorge warriors in boar's-tusk helmets. Another room in the house is decorated with a frieze of a repeated motif of the stern cabin of a ship.

Interpreting these frescoes at a distance of 3,500 years is hard, but ancient historian Fritz Schachermeyr takes a personal slant. He identifies the house with the fleet frescoes as belonging to the commander of such a fleet – the main fresco is an account of one of his journeys and the port shown is Akrotiri itself. Meanwhile, he has decorated his own bedroom with cabins because of their personal significance, while the two fishing youths in the parlour are his sons.

Schachermeyr also has an influential theory about Akrotiri as a whole. The absence of any palace buildings indicates that there was no ruling family. Rather, the nature of the houses (their size and quality) suggests that there were several rich families, possibly patricians, and the heterogeneous forms taken by the frescoes underline the way that taste and style were not defined by a central authority, but created on an individual basis. All this, he argues, points to Akrotiri being a maritime republic of the type seen throughout history, from Athens and Carthage, Genoa and Venice, to Hamburg and Bremen, Amsterdam and London. In such cities a prosperous merchant class was independent and liberal in governance and thought, and its society prospered as a result. Could Akrotiri have been the first such maritime republic?

ⓘ information

Location

Akrotiri
Santorini
Cyclades Islands
Greece

 Travel site
www.sacred-destinations.com/greece/santorini-akrotiri.htm

Transport

 Santorini

KNOSSOS

See map p.7 (12)

LOCATION:	CRETE, GREECE
CONSTRUCTED:	*c.*1900BCE
ABANDONED:	*c.*1380BCE
BUILT BY:	MINOANS
KEY FEATURES:	PALACE; CENTRAL COURT; FRESCOES; PIANO NOBILE; ROYAL APARTMENTS; LUSTRAL BASINS; PLUMBING AND FLUSHING TOILET

Homer's Odyssey, generally thought to be a chronicle of the heroes of mighty Bronze Age civilizations, describes Crete as 'a rich and lovely land, densely peopled and boasting 90 cities [including] a great city called Knossos…' Until 1900, few scholars believed that Crete had indeed hosted a Bronze Age civilization, but a few years of intensive excavation proved not only that the ancient epic had been right, but that Knossos was the centre of perhaps the first civilization in Europe.

Knossos on Crete was the site of the legendary Labyrinth of the Minotaur, constructed by King Minos and penetrated by the hero Theseus with the help of Minos's daughter Ariadne. A mound at a site in northern Crete called Kephala was traditionally identified as the site of Knossos and in the late 19th century, with interest in archaeology mounting and Schliemann making the headlines with his groundbreaking discoveries at Troy (see page 22), attention turned here.

In 1878, the first attempts at systematic excavation were made by a Cretan antiquarian appropriately named Minos Kalokairinos, but his efforts were limited by the Turkish occupation of the island. Schliemann himself was keen to excavate the site, but it was not until 1900, with the expulsion of the Turks, that British historian Arthur Evans was able to acquire the site and start digging in earnest. Evans had been inspired by Schliemann's discovery of Mycenae, which had pushed back the

◀ **Knossos Palace.** The buildings have been partially reconstructed, giving the modern visitor a sense of the vast scale of the original palace complex.

chronology of civilization in Europe by nearly a thousand years, and had also become intrigued by evidence for another Bronze Age Mediterranean civilization, in the form of clay seals marked with depictions of marine life, which were alien to Mycenae, Egypt or any other known culture, and that seemed to originate from Crete.

In just five years of archaeology, Evans peeled back the layers of the mound at Kephala to reveal an enormous structure, which he immediately identified as the Palace of Minos himself. Within were vivid frescoes, tablets inscribed with an unidentifiable language, sophisticated plumbing, well-crafted artefacts and treasures of gold and silver – all the trappings of a new and previously unknown civilization, whom Evans christened Minoans after the legendary king.

KNOSSOS THROUGH THE AGES

Over a century of archaeology at Knossos and other, similar sites around Crete, has revealed much about the history of the Minoans. The first settlements at Knossos date back to at least c.6000BCE, with urban civilization developing towards the end of the Early Bronze Age. In the period labelled the Middle Minoan, from about 1900BCE, Minoan architecture began to take shape and large buildings became a feature of settlements. Eventually these grew to become palace complexes. At least four major palace complexes have been found on Crete, with Knossos being the largest.

Archaeologists use the term 'palace complex' because these great structures were obviously much more than simply places of residence for kings or chieftains. They are equipped with extensive storage facilities, workshops, public spaces, cult shrines and ritual spaces, as well as what look like banqueting halls, audience rooms and suites of private chambers. They dominate the settlements of which they are the foci – the palace at Knossos had around 1,300 rooms, while the city around it was relatively small (although estimates of the population vary from as few as 5,000 to as many as 30,000 or even higher).

The palaces were the centre of Minoan life for 600 years, with Knossos lasting the longest. The Old Palace or First Palatial period, from 1900BCE, was cut short by a catastrophic earthquake that brought widespread destruction, but the palaces were rebuilt grander than before and Minoan civilization reached its apogee during the Neopalatial period. But around 1450BCE fresh disasters struck – probably more earthquakes, but possibly the eruption of Thera (see page 80). In the Postpalatial period most of the palaces except for Knossos were abandoned and the evidence from the types of pottery, writing and other cultural artefacts at the site suggests that it had been taken over by the Mycenaeans, the power that had been rising on the Greek mainland.

Around 1380BCE, Knossos was destroyed by fire and abandoned altogether, although what caused the fire is unclear. New settlements sprang up during Classical Greek and Roman times, but in the Middle Ages nearby towns supplanted Knossos and only local traditions connected it to the ancient legends.

THE PALACE OF KNOSSOS

Constructed on Crete's northern coast, Knossos was a vast palace complex. The floor area of one of its levels is around 13,000 square metres (139,000 square feet). Given that most of the palace consisted of at least two, and sometimes up to five storeys, the total floor area must have been at least double this. In all, there were around 1,300 rooms, with multiple kinked corridors, giving a truly labyrinthine dimension.

▼ **Palace location.** The palace was sited in the centre of the broad valley of the River Kairatos, about 8 kilometres (5 miles) from the sea, which was crucial for developing the Minoans' mercantile empire.

▲ **Dolphin fresco.** Although currently in the Queen's Megaron, recent research suggests that the fresco was originally painted on the floor of the room now known as the Treasury.

The palace was arranged as four wings set around a central court. The court possibly served as a public area — perhaps similar to a Greek *agora* or Roman forum — but may also have simply been a device to ensure maximum access to air and light.

The other possible use of the central court was as the arena for ceremonial sports. Decoration and motifs throughout the palace testify to the importance of the bull as a symbol to the Minoans, most famously in the context of frescoes showing 'bull leaping' — where young Minoans (both men and women) apparently faced an onrushing bull and somersaulted between its horns and over its back before landing on their feet behind it. Whether this actually took place, or was even possible, is unclear. The pictures may be purely symbolic.

The different wings or blocks around the court seem to have had separate functions. The lower floor of the west wing was mainly devoted to storerooms, known as magazines. These featured stone-lined pits to hold liquids and many large clay jars to hold other goods. Above these was an upper storey consisting of 'halls of state', possibly used for audiences, receptions or government business. Also in the west wing were cult rooms – cryptlike rooms with pillars marked with magical or arcane symbols. In particular the double-headed axe blade symbol beloved of the Minoans, and known as a *labrys* in Greek, from which the word labyrinth is derived, features. These symbols may have been intended to help appease the Earth gods and ward off earthquakes.

The east wing of the palace contained suites of rooms that were apparently residential quarters, including areas dubbed by Evans the 'apartments of King Minos', a bathroom with a lustral basin (a sunken bath thought to have had ritual/religious significance) and a toilet room, with arguably the world's earliest flushing toilet. Highly sophisticated plumbing was a major feature of the palace, with aqueducts bringing water and clay pipes carrying away sewage. These pipes were put together using standardized, mass-produced units that tapered along their length to produce a waterproof seal.

MINOAN MYSTERIES

Despite the evidence of Knossos and the dozens of other sites on Crete, the Minoan civilization remains hedged with mysteries. What were its roots? How much inspiration did it draw from the cultures of Egypt, Assyria and the Levant? Was Minoan civilization really a peace-loving, non-militaristic, utopian paradise, as suggested by the general absence of weapons or militaristic art? Or was there a sinister underside of human sacrifice, as suggested by some remains found at Minoan cult sites and by the sinister legend of the Minotaur?

Light might be shed on these issues if Minoan language and writing were not also impenetrable mysteries. Clay tablets found at Knossos are inscribed with a script known as Linear A, which seems to encode a language unrelated to any known language making it impossible to decipher.

 ## information

Location

Knossos

Crete

Greece

 Travel site

www.sacred-destinations. com/greece/knossos

Transport

 Heraklion

AFRICA

The five cities in this chapter span a vast gulf of history, from the 11th century BCE to the 15th century CE. But they also span a cultural gulf, between the super-Saharan world of the famous civilizations of antiquity and the sub-Saharan world that remains little known and poorly understood. The former is the familiar world of the ancient Egyptians, Greeks and Romans, in which the extraordinarily long narrative of Egyptian history, represented here through the tale of the lost city of Tanis, gives way to the Classical world, and the famous names of Alexandria, a Greek city with an Egyptian flavour, and Leptis Magna, one of the best preserved of all Roman cities.

The haunting site of Great Zimbabwe offers a rare window onto the untold history of the sub-Saharan world, although it took the efforts of unbiased and professional archaeologists to start to unravel its mystery, for, like several sites covered in this book (see, for instance, Cahokia on page 148 and Tiwanaku on page 174), it has been subject to interpretation (or misinterpretation) through ideologically rather than scientifically motivated research.

The two worlds are bridged by the ancient city of Meroe and the venerable Kushite civilization of which it was the capital. The Kushites are rarely seen as much more than adjuncts to their more famous neighbour to the north, Egypt, but in practice they represent a coming together of the super- and sub-Saharan worlds. Initially they developed in imitation of the Egyptians, but the establishment of Meroe signalled a geopolitical shift towards the sub-Saharan world and the development of a new, uniquely sub-Saharan culture.

Granite sphinx and Pompey's Pillar. At the ancient fort of Rhakotis in Alexandria, ▶
Egypt. Pompey's Pillar, a 88-foot (27-metre) high marble column dating from the
2nd century CE, was actually dedicated to Diocletian soon after 297CE.

LEPTIS MAGNA

See map p.7 (13)

LOCATION:	LIBYA
CONSTRUCTED:	1000BCE
ABANDONED:	c.6TH CENTURY CE
BUILT BY:	PHOENICIANS; ROMANS
KEY FEATURES:	ARCH OF SEVERUS; ARCH OF TRAJAN; AMPHITHEATRE; CIRCUS; THEATRE; VILLAS AND MOSAICS

One of the best preserved of all ancient Roman cities is Leptis Magna (also Lepcis Magna), on the coast of what is now Libya, 130 kilometres (81 miles) east of Tripoli. In its heyday it was the third most important city in Africa, after Alexandria and Carthage. The remains of a range of public buildings, particularly of the theatre, amphitheatre and a magnificent arch erected in honour of the city's most famous son, the emperor Septimius Severus, bear testament to the splendour of the city in its heyday. Of particular significance are the discoveries of exquisite mosaics at luxury villas on the outskirts of Leptis, which rank among the greatest Roman works of art ever produced.

CROSSROADS BY THE SEA

Although best known as a Roman city, Leptis Magna long predated the Romans.

Initially founded around 1000BCE as a Phoenician city, possibly on the site of a pre-existing Berber settlement (the Berbers were the indigenous peoples of the region), it later fell within the orbit of Carthage, the trading empire with its own roots in Phoenicia. But Carthage clashed with Rome, suffering catastrophic defeat in the Second Punic War; the victors forced it to restrict its sphere of influence and Leptis increasingly became an independent city. After Carthage's final obliteration in the Third Punic War in 146BCE, it fell to the Roman client king, Massinissa of Numidia, and then into the orbit of Rome, and was finally formally incorporated into the empire in the reign of Tiberius (14–37CE).

Leptis Magna. A wealth of well-preserved remains can ▶ be found here as most of the city was constructed from high-quality, erosion-resistant hard limestone.

▲ **Hadrianic baths.** The impressive baths were commissioned by Emperor Hadrian in the 2nd century CE.

The Phoenicians had probably chosen to site a colony here because of Wadi Lebda, the seasonal river that reaches the coast at this point, providing a source of water in an otherwise largely arid region. Later it would gain greater economic significance as a waypoint along the coastal highway that ran from Alexandria through Cyrene to the refounded Roman colony of Carthage. As well as trans-African trade, Leptis was a major exporter of grain and olive oil to Rome and a shipping point for the exotic animals demanded by the circuses of Rome.

ROMAN RULE

Under Roman rule Leptis Magna became increasingly prosperous. During the reign of the Emperor Trajan (98–117CE), the city was granted *colonia* status, being renamed *Colonia Ulpia Traiana Lepcitanorium*. This conferred major economic and political advantages – for instance, all free-born male inhabitants became full Roman citizens.

Trajan was succeeded by Hadrian, whose taste for marble influenced the subsequent look of the city and under whose governance major new hydrological works were

leaders, with civil war, barbarian invasion and economic turmoil in what is known by historians as the Crisis of the 3rd Century. The population declined and by the 4th century the city was weak and vulnerable to Berber raids. Worse was to come, with a massive earthquake in 365CE levelling many buildings. In 455CE rampaging Vandals, pillaging their way through North Africa, conquered Leptis and tore down its walls, a move that was to prove short-sighted. The Vandals settled down and established a kingdom based around Carthage, but Leptis had been left vulnerable and was razed in a devastating Berber attack in 523CE, from which it never recovered.

Eleven years later the Byzantine general Belisarius destroyed the Vandal kingdom, recaptured Leptis and rebuilt the city, but on a much smaller scale. Although it was designated the provincial capital, Leptis had suffered too much and by the time of the Arab invasion in the mid-7th century, the city was almost deserted but for its garrison of Byzantine soldiers.

instituted. A new aqueduct was constructed to bring water overland from Wadi Camm, 19 kilometres (12 miles) away. This additional supply helped to feed the new public baths complex – one of the largest outside of Rome – completed in 127CE.

But the heyday of Leptis Magna was yet to come, under Septimius Severus (r. 193–211CE), who initiated a major programme of public works. This marked the zenith of Leptis Magna's fortunes, for the stability of Severan rule was soon followed by a succession of weak and divided

ROUGH GUIDE TO LEPTIS MAGNA

Only a portion of the site has been excavated, but many impressive ruins still stand. The basic plan of the city reflects its old and new parts, both with gridlike street patterns, but with the original Punic city at a slightly different orientation to the later

Roman expansion. The main axis of the Roman city was the Cardo Maximus, the main street, which ran from the old market area in the north-east to intersect with the main coast road. The latter formed the city's Decumanus (the other primary axis).

At the junction of these two main roads is one of the most impressive monuments to be seen in Leptis Magna, the Arch of Severus. The arch is unusual in being a *tetrapylon* or *quadrifrons* – i.e. having four pillars and four arches. Although the current arch is a reconstruction from the 1920s, archaeologists have been able to determine that it was probably adapted from a pre-existing structure and that it seemed to have taken as long as eight years to complete, with work starting, halting and then being rapidly completed in anticipation of Severus's visit to the city in 203CE.

Along the Cardo Maximus to the north-east is the Arch of Trajan. To the left

▼ **Roman frieze.** From the magnificent triumphal arch of Septimus Severus, who initiated an ambitious building programme at Leptis Magna, this frieze shows oxen being sacrificed.

of this, partially cut into a hill, is the city's theatre, the oldest and second largest in Roman Africa, built around 1 or 2CE. Until the construction of the amphitheatre, it may have been used to stage gladiatorial combats. It features a temple, possibly constructed here to circumvent Roman strictures on theatres as immoral – with a temple on site the building became sacred and could not be torn down. To the south-east of the Cardo is the Severan Basilica, or law courts, which became a church in Byzantine times. At its north-eastern end the Cardo led to the Old Forum, the oldest part of town where the original Punic settlement was centred. To the east of this was the harbour, including port buildings and even a lighthouse – a smaller replica of the great one at Alexandria (see page 108).

A kilometre to the east of the city lie the amphitheatre and circus. Little is left of the latter, which sat where the beach is today, but in ancient times it could seat up to 25,000 people, who came to watch chariot races and other sports. The amphitheatre,

however, is largely intact. With seating for 16,000 people and an oval arena measuring 57 x 47 metres (187 x 154 feet).

VILLAS FIT FOR PRINCES

Some of the most remarkable finds have come from the surrounding countryside, where rich citizens lived in luxurious villas and displayed their wealth and taste through exquisite mosaics, some of which have survived. In 2000, the best mosaic yet was uncovered by archaeologists from the University of Hamburg, lining the cold plunge pool of the bathhouse of a villa to the south of Leptis. The mosaic shows an exhausted gladiator, taking a breather while surveying his defeated opponent.

However, controversy erupted over the decision to cut the mosaic out from its site and transplant it to the local museum. Detractors claim that the operation was clumsy and damaged the mosaic, but defenders insist it was the best move and point to wider problems with low levels of funding in Libyan archaeology and heritage.

---

 information

Location

Leptis Magna
District of Khoms
Libya

 UNESCO site
whc.unesco.org/en/list/183

Transport

 Tripoli

TANIS

See map p.7 (14)

LOCATION:	NILE DELTA, EGYPT
CONSTRUCTED:	*c.*1070 BCE
ABANDONED:	PRE-7TH CENTURY CE
BUILT BY:	PHARAOH SMENDES AND THE TWENTY-FIRST AND TWENTY-SECOND DYNASTIES
KEY FEATURES:	TEMPLE COMPOUND; TEMPLE OF AMUN; ROYAL TOMBS

Scattered blocks and the stumps of obelisks litter the top of a huge sand mound, marooned along the former course of a long-since silted-up branch of the Nile Delta. Here was the site of Tanis, one-time capital of ancient Egypt and the site of the only authentically undisturbed royal tombs, the extraordinary contents of which rival the glories of Tutankhamun.

Tanis is the Greek name for the ancient Egyptian city of Djanet, a site known today as San el-Hagar – 'the place of stones'. Technically speaking, San el-Hagar actually refers to the northernmost and larger of two huge sand mounds, or *gezira*: it rises over 30 metres (98½ feet) above the surrounding flood plain and has an area of 177 hectares (437 acres). From around the 11th century

BCE until the late 8th century BCE, it was the capital of Egypt (albeit one of several at some points). Before and after this, it was an important regional capital and a major religious and trading centre, funnelling trans-Mediterranean trade into and out of Egypt, until its branch of the Nile silted up and it was left high and dry.

DELTA PHARAOHS AND SOUTHERN HIGH PRIESTS

Tanis was the product of a confused and divisive period of ancient Egyptian politics. The Twentieth Dynasty was weak and failing and in Upper Egypt (the southern part of the country) the pharaoh had lost most real power to the high priests of Amun in the city of Thebes. By the end of the reign of

◀ **Bas relief.** This relief depicts verses from the *Book of the Dead* in the royal tomb of Shoshenq III at Tanis dating from around 883BC. Horus the falcon god is shown holding the fetish of Abydos.

Ramesses XI, last pharaoh of the Twentieth Dynasty, the High Priest Herihor was openly sharing power as co-ruler. The rise of the high priests saw the pharaonic power base shift to the north of Egypt in the Nile Delta region, where the city of Pi-Ramesses had been made the capital. At the death of Ramesses XI, the throne passed to the governor of Tanis, one Smendes, who may have been Ramesses' son-in-law. He chose Tanis as his residence, superseding Pi-Ramesses, whose own branch of the Nile was now drying up.

Smendes's Twenty-First Dynasty had Libyan connections, which became more marked with the transition to the Twenty-Second Dynasty under Shoshenq I, which retained Tanis as its seat. However, in the mid-9th century BCE the south of Egypt broke away to become a separate kingdom, and by the 8th century BCE several rival dynasties were established, running concurrently and each ruling a portion of Egypt; Tanis was now only the capital of a small local kingdom. Egypt was reunited by a Nubian dynasty around 720BCE (see Meroe page 112), and Tanis henceforth reverted to the role of a provincial capital.

With only intermittent control of the country and much civil strife, the view of the dynasties of the Third Intermediate Period has traditionally been that they were poor shadows of former glories, scraping by in pale imitation of the wealth and opulent splendour of the preceding New Kingdom. Discoveries made at Tanis were to both reinforce and undermine this accepted view.

DECODING TANIS

When French Egyptologist Pierre Montet began what was to be the most significant exploration of the site in 1929, he uncovered inscriptions and statues that seemed to identify the site as the lost city of Avaris, which was later renamed Pi-Ramesses. But later Egyptologists have realized that Montet and his predecessors were wrong and that the inscriptions were misleading: the blocks and statuary were moved from elsewhere. It is now clear that the nearby, but probably largely abandoned, city of Pi-Ramesses had served as a sort of quarry for the builders of Tanis. Other blocks, obelisks and statues came from other locations. Some dated back as far as the Old Kingdom. This evidence of a capital cobbled together from the recycled detritus of older cities would appear to tie in with the traditional view of the impoverished Intermediate dynasties. However, it may have been that the northern delta kings did not have access to the quarries of Upper Egypt when they built their new capital and were simply being practical.

Excavations have revealed that the primary feature of the city was a huge wall

of
mud
brick, which
enclosed a sandy bowl
between four raised areas on the San el-
Hagar mound, creating a huge temple
compound. The wall was 10 metres (33 feet)
high and 15 metres (49 feet) thick. It was
built by Psusennes I, third pharaoh of the
Twenty-First Dynasty (r. 1039–991BCE),
in an apparent effort to create a northern
Thebes. Thebes was the religious capital
of Egypt, with a complex of temples to the
'divine family' – Amun, Mut and Khonsu.
Its importance as the focus of Egyptian
religious and cultural life brought power
and prestige. Psusennes created his own
temple complex with shrines to the divine
family and then went further and created
a northern analogue of Thebes's Valley of
the Kings – the sacred valley where the great
pharaohs of ages past had been interred.

Other structures that have been
identified include smaller temples (chapels)

▲ **Falcon collar.** One of the gold treasures discovered at
Tanis, this collar belonged to Shoshenq I, c.945–925BCE.

built by later pharaohs. After the Persian
occupation of Egypt (525–405BCE),
Nectanebo I of the Thirtieth Dynasty
(r. 380–362BCE) initiated a programme of
building at Tanis. He built a new, enormous
mud-brick enclosure and additional temples,
as well as constructing a sacred lake in the
northern corner of the city. Egypt soon fell
again to the Persians and then to Alexander
the Great and afterwards was ruled by the

▲ **Statue of Ramesses II.** A large statue of Ramesses II and the Tanite Triad (the chief deities worshipped at Tanis were Amun, his consort, Mur and their child Khonsu) at the Temple of Amun, Tanis.

Greco–Egyptian Ptolemies. They completed some of these unfinished temples, but by now the original great temple to Amun was gone, its site built over with houses.

The Ptolemies gave way to the Romans, but by the end of the Roman Era the branch of the Nile that gave Tanis its raison d'être had silted up and it was largely abandoned by the time of the Islamic conquest. Lime burners destroyed much of the fabric of the city, leaving little but the granite blocks and obelisks that litter the site today.

TOMBS TO RIVAL TUTANKHAMUN

The unprepossessing detritus of ancient Tanis on the surface concealed something spectacular beneath. In 1939, in his eleventh season of excavation at Tanis, and with the gathering clouds of war in faraway Europe casting a long shadow over his endeavours, Montet unearthed a tomb within the temple precinct. Inscriptions identified it as that of Osorkon II (ruler during the Twenty-Second Dynasty 872–837BCE) and although it had been long plundered, the thieves had left behind heavy objects such as a stunning quartzite sarcophagus, *shabtis* (tomb statues supposed to come to life in the afterlife as servants for the dead pharaoh) and alabaster jars for his internal organs.

The adjoining tomb, which had not been disturbed, was far more impressive. Nested within a granite sarcophagus and a granite coffin was a coffin of solid silver; within lay incredible jewellery and a glorious face mask of solid gold (the mummy itself had largely decomposed). Although the inscriptions on the wall attributed the tomb to Psusennes I, who had originally built it for himself and his queen Mutnodjmet, there were numerous other burials in the five-chambered tomb, including three more Twenty-First Dynasty pharaohs, General Wendebauenjed (a key military man), and the previously unknown pharaoh Shoshenq II (ruler during Twenty-Second Dynasty), who occupied an unusual silver coffin with a head shaped like a falcon.

In all, Montet discovered six tombs, which hosted the burials of at least 14 royals and nobles. The exquisite treasures, including face masks of workmanship at least as fine as that of Tutankhamun, and fabulous jewellery of gold and lapis lazuli show that the kings of the Intermediate Period were far from impoverished. Yet the tombs also show the continuing practice of reusing materials. Sarcophagus lids were carved from statues, while a huge granite block used to plug the entrance to one of the tombs had originally been part of an obelisk in praise of Ramesses II. The use of a sarcophagus from Thebes reminds us that Psusennes's brother was High Priest at Thebes and was apparently responsible for state-sanctioned looting of the Valley of the Kings. Today, the wonders of Tanis sit in Cairo Museum.

A BBC documentary, broadcast in 2011, featured the work of US archaeologist Sarah Parcak, who uses infra-red satellite images of Egypt to look for ancient remains buried beneath the sand. The images of Tanis revealed a sprawling city of mud-brick buildings, four times larger in area than previously thought.

(i) information

Location

Tanis

Near San el-Hagur

Eastern Delta

Egypt

 National Geographic site

www.nationalgeographic.com/guides/history/ancient/tanis-egypt.html

Transport

 Cairo

 Faqus

ALEXANDRIA

See map p.7 (15)

LOCATION:	NILE DELTA, EGYPT
CONSTRUCTED:	331BCE
ABANDONED:	NOT ABANDONED
BUILT BY:	ALEXANDER THE GREAT; PTOLEMAIC PHARAOHS
KEY FEATURES:	LIGHTHOUSE OF PHAROS; LIBRARY; SERAPEUM; CATACOMBS OF KOM EL SHOQAFA

Known as the 'Pearl of the Mediterranean', Alexandria was one of the greatest and most remarkable cities in the world for a thousand years. It was a place of contradictions – a city of great learning and fundamentalist bigotry; cosmopolitan in the extreme and intolerant in the extreme; the greatest Greek city in history, but Egyptian; home to several Wonders of the World, including the Lighthouse, the Great Library, Alexander's Tomb and the Catacombs of Kom el Shoqafa.

CITY ON THE EDGE

On Egypt's Mediterranean coast, on a strip of land between Lake Mareotis and the sea, lies Egypt's second city and its largest port, Alexandria. The modern city bears few traces of the ancient metropolis that in its heyday was one of the largest cities in the world and arguably the greatest. It was founded by and named after Alexander the

Great. Having conquered Egypt and desirous of consolidating his power and reinforcing maritime and trade links between the Nile Valley and Greece and Asia, he chose one of the few suitable harbour sites on the Mediterranean coast, renowned enough for its natural advantages to be mentioned by Homer in the *Odyssey*. Book Four records that, 'Therein is a harbour with good anchorage, whence men launch the shapely ships into the sea…' The island of Pharos just offshore shielded the coast, while it was far enough away from the mouths of the Nile to be free of silt.

A small Egyptian town called Rhakotis occupied part of the site, but in around 331BCE Alexander marked out the basic

The Catacombs of Kom el Shoqafa. In the Rhakotis ▶
Quarter of Alexandria, the catacombs display a mix
of Egyptian, Greek and Roman influences.

layout of a new city – according to legend using grain when other materials were not available, such was his eagerness to get the project started – and employed the architect Dinocrates to elaborate. The city was laid out in classical Greek style, with orthogonal streets (running at right angles to give a grid pattern) oriented to the shoreline and based around two main axes: the east–west Canopus Street, running from the Moon Gate in the east to the Sun Gate in the west and the north–south Soma Street, running from Lake Mareotis to the shore, at a point where a causeway called the Heptastadion was built to link Pharos to the mainland and create a harbour on each side.

Alexander did not stay to see his city built, setting off for fresh adventures and conquests and dying in Babylon in 323BCE. Africa and the prize kingdom of Egypt were ultimately seized by his general, Ptolemy, thus founding the Ptolemaic Dynasty that was to shape Alexandria.

As the capital of the Hellenistic rulers of Egypt, Alexandria had a unique character from the start. It was Greek in design and many other aspects, with a mixed population of Greeks from across the Hellenistic world, Egyptians, Jews and, later in its history, Romans. Its iconography, culture and religions were highly syncretic – for instance, statues in tombs are Egyptian in style but with Roman clothing and hairstyles. There are many depictions of the Hellenistic Ptolemies in Egyptian idioms, such as sphinxes bearing their heads. Ancient Egyptian statues, obelisks and other structures were brought to Alexandria from other sites, as with Tanis (see page 100). Yet for all this, Alexandria was emphatically not Egyptian. It was often described as *Alexandria ad Aegyptum*, meaning 'Alexandria-adjoining-Egypt', and in Roman times the local governor bore the title 'Prefect of Alexandria and Egypt'.

Alexandria was the epicentre of trade for the Mediterranean world, well situated to take advantages of the trade routes from the Red Sea and Arabia that linked the Greco–Roman world to the Persian, Indian and Chinese worlds. It had the world's largest library and academic faculty, and its institutions attracted many of the world's great scholars, including Euclid (of geometry fame), Eratosthenes (who calculated the circumference of the Earth) and Aristarchus (who posited a heliocentric solar system). It was in Alexandria that the Old Testament was first translated into Greek, helping to fix its form thereafter.

HIGHLIGHTS OF ANCIENT ALEXANDRIA
Perhaps the most famous building in Alexandria was the Lighthouse, built

▲ **Roman theatre.** Uncovered in 1959, the Roman theatre is well-preserved and features sections of mosaic flooring.

on the eastern tip of the island of Pharos (although deposition either side of the Heptastadion means that Pharos is now part of the mainland). The Lighthouse was one of the Seven Wonders of the Ancient World, a great tower over 100 metres (328 feet) tall, with a fire and a giant mirror at the top to help guide ships into port. The main port was the Great Harbour to the east, while to the west of the Heptastadion was the Eunostos ('safe return') Harbour.

The Great Harbour curved round in a semicircle; at its eastern lip, a promontory called Cape Lochias was the location for the Ptolemaic palace complex, and around this the Bruchion, or Royal Quarter, where the Greek population was based, and which occupied the north-eastern third of central Alexandria. Here were the most magnificent buildings, including the Museum, a temple to the Muses, which was a sort of ancient academy, hosting a

THE LIBRARY OF ALEXANDRIA

The library has become a legendary place, and its destruction has become the archetype of cultural vandalism, described as 'the day that history lost its memory'. It was said to contain more than 500,000 books. In practice, however, the Great Library's size has probably been exaggerated — a building that could hold this many books would have needed some 40 kilometres (25 miles) of shelving, but there is no hint in historical descriptions of Alexandria of a building colossal enough to host this. Comparison with other ancient libraries, in conjunction with other clues, suggests a more realistic figure in the tens rather than hundreds of thousands.

The destruction of the library has also become shrouded in legend. Several culprits are blamed. Julius Caesar accidentally set fire to a large portion of the city when besieged by a mob in 47BCE; a Christian mob under Patriarch Theophilus razed pagan temples in 391CE and Muslim forces that conquered Egypt in 640CE supposedly burned the books to heat the city's bathhouses. Most likely there was not a single destructive event, but several, culminating in the library's ruin.

permanent staff of scholars and scribes and attracting the famous names mentioned above. Next to, or possibly inside, the Museum was the Royal Library, also known as the Great Library of Alexandria (see box above).

To the east of the Royal Quarter was the large Jewish quarter, which ruled itself as a semi-autonomous enclave. In the centre of the harbour were the Navalia, or docks, and behind them the Emporium, or Exchange and the Apostases, or Magazines. Also in this area were two temples – the Timonium, built by Mark Antony, and the Caesarium – and two obelisks, later known as Cleopatra's Needles and removed to London and New York.

Among the numerous other temples the most notable were temples to Isis and Serapis. Isis was a traditional Egyptian goddess redefined to a much wider role as a sort of Greco–Roman super-goddess, while Serapis was a Ptolemaic invention, a combination of the Egyptian gods Osiris and Apis (the sacred bull god) designed specifically to give Alexandria a patron deity and provide the disparate Greek and Egyptian inhabitants with a common religious focus. The Serapeum, the main temple in Alexandria, was sited on a rocky outcrop in the south of the city, with 100 steps leading up to it. Among other functions, it also served as an auxiliary or 'daughter' library to the main, or Royal

Library. West of the Serapeum was located one of Alexandria's many cemeteries, now known as the Catacombs of Kom el Shoqafa, a remarkable confluence of Egyptian custom and style with Greek and Roman influences. This part of town was the Rhakotis Quarter, where the Egyptians lived.

DECLINE AND FALL

Under the Romans, Alexandria became the second city in the empire, but it also became increasingly fractious and violent. Tensions between the city's ethnic groups flared up regularly, with pogroms against the Jews, for instance, while Roman emperors such as Caracalla visited destruction and massacres on the city. The ascendancy of Christianity, which made Alexandria into one of the leading centres of the early Church, simply added to the tensions, culminating in vicious anti-pagan rampages by the patriarch Theophilus in 391CE, when he led a mob that razed the Serapeum, and his nephew Cyril, who was responsible for the death of the pagan mathematician and philosopher Hypatia in 412CE. Severe earthquakes also took their toll and the city was much diminished when conquered by the Arabs in 640CE, although it was still magnificent enough for General Amr ibn al-As to report back to Caliph Omar that the city had '4,000 palaces, 4,000 baths and 400 theatres'.

Changes in trade routes and the establishment of a new capital by the Muslims caused Alexandria to dwindle still further, so that by the 18th century it was only a small town. Earthquakes, subsidence and rising sea levels meant that most of the Royal Quarter had slipped beneath the waves and only since the mid-1990s has underwater archaeology started to rediscover its remains. For the Georgian sightseer, Alexandria was a tremendous disappointment. James Bruce reported in 1768 that 'now we can say of [Alexandria], as of Carthage, *periere ruinae*. Even its ruins have disappeared'.

 ## information

Location

Roman Amphitheatre
Alexandria
Egypt

 World Guides site
www.alexandria.world-guides.com/alexandria_landmarks.html

Transport

 Burg al-Arab

 Misr

MEROE

See map p.7 16

LOCATION: SUDAN
CONSTRUCTED: c.750BCE
ABANDONED: c.350CE
BUILT BY: KUSHITES
KEY FEATURES: PYRAMIDS; TEMPLES OF AMUN AND
APADEMAK; ROYAL BATHS; BRONZE
HEAD OF AUGUSTUS

The Kingdom of Kush had chosen Meroe as its capital for much of its history. It is a city fabled by ancient authors and marked by its distinctive pyramids and exotic tomb treasures, but which met its end in an industrial–ecological crisis that offers a stark warning to our modern world.

THE LAND OF KUSH

The kingdom to the south of ancient Egypt has gone by many different names, but is best known as Kush (sometimes Cush). Here along the upper reaches of the Nile, from the First Cataract down to the far south, in what is now Sudan, Africans built a long-lasting civilization that both drew inspiration from and contended with Egypt.

Meroe's distinctive pyramids. The steep angles of Meroe's pyramids drew inspiration from the Egyptian private tombs of the New Kingdom (1550–1070BCE).

The first Kushite kingdom from around 2400BCE centred on Kerma. It was able to flourish during a period of relative instability and weakness in its powerful neighbour, but when new dynasties re-established control over Egypt they also regained their dominance over the lands to the south. Later phases of Kushite development saw its centre shift further away from Egypt and towards sub-Saharan Africa, initially geographically when the Egyptians reasserted control and moved the capital south to Napata, and later culturally as well, when the capital eventually moved to Meroe.

The collapse of the New Kingdom and the disarray of Egypt's Third Intermediate Period (see Tanis page 100) once again allowed Kush to develop as an independent kingdom, with its capital at Napata and a dynastic cemetery established at the nearby site of El-Kurru. The power of this Napatan kingdom grew until Nubian kings were dictating terms to the Egyptians, culminating in Kushites taking complete control of Egypt and establishing the Twenty-Fifth Dynasty, which ruled, at first in tandem with northern dynasties and later in sole power, from 747–656BCE.

THE RISE OF MEROE
Invasion by the Assyrians and later, re-establishment of native Egyptian dynasty,

forced the Kushites back into their own lands and attempts by Kushite kings to reconquer territory to the north were repulsed. From around 750BCE the city of Meroe, on the east bank of the Nile, about 200 kilometres (124 miles) north-east of modern-day Khartoum, had become an important administrative centre for the south of Kush. When the Egyptian pharaoh Psametik II raided far into Kushite territory in 591BCE, sacking Napata, its strategic

▼ **The Temple of Apademak.** This temple was built by King Natekamani and Queen Amanitore to pay homage to Apademak (the lion god) – god of war and fertility.

benefits became more obvious. The Kushite King Aspelta relocated the royal court to Meroe and it remained the capital of Kush until around 350CE.

A rich and powerful city far to the south of territory familiar to the Egyptians and the successive masters of Egypt – the Persians, the Greeks and eventually the Romans – Meroe became a fabled land. The Persian emperor Cambyses sent a huge expeditionary force up the Nile, lured by the promise of great booty, but it turned back, defeated by the harsh terrain. Classical writers such as Herodotus and Diodorus Siculus spoke of Meroe in terms of wonder. It was said to sit on a great island in the Nile, possibly reflecting the fact that in reality it was surrounded on three sides by water.

CITY OF INDUSTRY

One of the economic foundations of Kush was its iron industry. It was rich in ore and manufactured iron for export as well as domestic use. Meroe was the centre of iron smelting, supplied with water from the Nile and, crucially, a rich source of wood for charcoal production in the form of dense acacia groves. It has been described as the 'Birmingham of ancient Africa', attested to by ancient slag heaps, such as the one on which Meroe's Lion Temple sits.

In the early days of Kush, trade depended on the Nile, which gave access to the

AMANIRENAS

The Kushite kandake *Amanirenas was a formidable queen and also a courageous general. When the Romans imposed their control on the stretch of the Nile between Egypt and Kush, Amanirenas and her son led an army north to capture the territory, enslave the populace and carry off the statue of Augustus. In defending Kush against Gaius Petronius's expedition she lost an eye, but succeeded in halting the Roman advance. Eventually the Romans were forced to sue for peace. According to legend, they presented him with a bundle of arrows and the message, 'The* kandake *sends you these arrows. If you want peace they are a token of her friendship and warmth. If you want war, you are going to need them.'*

Mediterranean, but as its centre shifted south, so new trade routes independent of Egypt opened up. The growth of trade routes along the Red Sea, mediated by Greek and Nabataean merchants (see Petra page 46), cut out the need to travel via the Nile, while the increasing use of camels from the 2nd century BCE opened caravan routes extending across the whole of sub-Saharan Africa. Meroe became part of a lucrative trade network stretching from West Africa to India and China.

▲ **Temple of Amon.** This monumental sculpture of a ram is part of a group of 12 identical statues that form the alley leading to the Temple of Amon.

PYRAMIDS

The Kushites adopted the Egyptian practice of using pyramids as royal tombs, but based the style on the private tombs of the New Kingdom (1550–1070BCE), rather than the royal pyramids of Egypt's Old and Middle Kingdoms (27th to 17th centuries BCE).

When the tombs were excavated in the 19th and early 20th centuries, no mummies were found (they may not have survived or the Kushites may not have practised mummification), but rich troves of grave goods were uncovered. Most spectacular of all were the finds of the treasure hunter Giuseppe Ferlini in 1834, who destroyed many pyramids in his hunt for loot, but successfully uncovered the tomb treasures of Queen Amanishakheto, including much exquisitely crafted jewellery.

After the capital moved to Meroe, Kushite culture became increasingly African and the tomb treasures of Meroe help to illustrate this cultural evolution. According to Dr Salah el-Din Muhammed Ahmed, director of fieldwork at the National Museum in Khartoum, 'From the graves and images painted on tombs we can see that people looked much more African than Mediterranean. The jewellery is of an African nature and you can still find the style of the jewellery used by the Meroites on tribes of the savannah belt south of Khartoum.'

THE LINE OF QUEENS

One of the most intriguing features of ancient Meroitic Kush was the importance of its queens, known via the Greeks as *kandakes*, which in turn was mistaken as the personal name 'Candace' by some ancient writers. The *kandake* shared power with a *qore*, or king, but he was often a purely ceremonial figure, while his consort was commander-in-chief, prime minister and chief priestess. One famous legend tells of how Alexander the Great led his armies to the walls of Meroe but halted and turned back when confronted by Queen Candace and her legions.

THE END OF MEROE

Exactly what happened to Meroe is unclear. Traditionally, it was thought that the rising power of the kingdom of Aksum (also Axum) in Ethiopia led to the decline of Kush and that Meroe fell to the invading Akumsite king Ezana *c.* 350CE. A *stele* erected at Meroe bears testament to his triumph. But it is now generally believed that Meroe was already largely abandoned by this time and that by then the region was mainly inhabited by the pastoral Noba tribe. So what happened to the glories of Meroe and its thriving population?

Historians now suspect that Meroe's iron industry was the true culprit. Extensive deforestation to produce the charcoal needed to fire the furnaces may have led to ecological collapse. Top soil eroded, rainfall declined and the region became arid and unproductive. In combination with the failure of the trade routes and pressure from the Noba, this was too much for Meroitic Kush and it collapsed.

 information

Location

Meroe

Begrawiya

Sudan

 Travel site

www.addictedtotravel.com/travel-guides/places-to-visit/meroe_sudan-travel-guide

Transport

 Khartoum

GREAT ZIMBABWE

See map p.7 (17)

LOCATION: ZIMBABWE
CONSTRUCTED: *c.*13TH CENTURY CE
ABANDONED: LATE 15TH CENTURY CE
BUILT BY: MWENE MUTAPA EMPIRE
KEY FEATURES: GREAT ENCLOSURE; SOPHISTICATED DRY-STONE MASONRY; CONICAL TOWER; HILLTOP COMPLEX; STONE BIRDS

The greatest archaeological site in sub-Saharan Africa and perhaps the only one to lend its name to a modern-day state, Great Zimbabwe was once the centre of a mighty trading empire.

Great Zimbabwe's most prominent feature is a circular wall known as the Great Enclosure, a feat of sophisticated monumental masonry that continues to awe and inspire today as it must have when it was first constructed, probably during the 13th–15th centuries CE.

This was the height of the Mwene Mutapa Empire (known by Europeans as Monomotapa), a kingdom of the Shona (who still live in the area) that developed from about 900CE. At first the empire was based on cattle herding, but from around

1100CE Mwene Mutapa took over control of the lucrative trading networks that linked ivory, iron and gold production centres inland with the merchants on the coast, who brought in return luxury goods from the Middle and Far East. Goods found at the site include silk, cotton, Chinese porcelain, Persian faience, glass from Syria and beads from India. In particular, rich gold fields were opened up to the west of Great Zimbabwe and considerable wealth flowed through the hands of the king, or *mambo*.

THE HILL COMPLEX

The whole complex covers about 728 hectares (1,800 acres), but the ruins are concentrated at three main sites. Atop a rocky hill sits the group of ruins known

Majestic location. The site of Great Zimbabwe was built across a valley and adjoining hills on the ▶ Zimbabwe Plateau – a region of high ground between the Zambezi and Limpopo rivers in southern Africa.

▲ **The Great Enclosure.** Located below the Hill Complex, the Great Enclosure is encircled by a giant wall with a circumference of 244 metres (735 feet). No mortar was used to hold together the stone blocks.

as the Hill Complex, which includes an oval stone enclosure about 100 metres (330 feet) across at its widest point and up to 11 metres (36 feet) high, within which sit a number of huts and small buildings made of *daga* – mud, gravel and earth from termite mounds, mixed to give a sort of concrete, which forms the most common building material in Africa. Remains indicate that it was first settled by Iron Age herders and farmers as early as the 5th century CE,

probably attracted by the area's rich grazing, fertile soil and, thanks to its altitude, relative lack of tsetse-fly spreading sleeping sickness. When Great Zimbabwe became rich, the Hill Complex was developed into the enclave of the *mambo* and possibly other figures of power, such as priests. A number of stone birds perched on top of stone pillars were found inside the complex, one of which has since become the national emblem of Zimbabwe.

THE GREAT ENCLOSURE

Below the Hill Complex is the most iconic and impressive of Great Zimbabwe's wonders – the Great Enclosure, known by the 19th-century residents of the area as the *Imbahuru*, which means either 'great house' or 'house of the great woman' in the local Karanga dialect of Shona. This latter translation would prove to have significant resonance for early European interpretations of the site. The Great Enclosure is an elliptical space enclosed by a giant wall with a circumference of 244 metres (735 feet), which is up to 11 metres (33 feet) high in places. It is constructed of two layers of rectangular granite blocks, laid together with such precision that no mortar was required, filled with earth and stones. Almost one million blocks were used in its construction.

Notable features of the Great Enclosure include an inner wall that runs around part of the main wall to create a 55-metre (180-foot) long alley, with openings and doorways, smoothly rounded walls and rounded steps crafted with great skill. Inside the enclosure is a solid conical tower 9 metres (30 feet) high, a number of standing stones and traces of many *daga* huts.

THE VALLEY RUINS

Scattered throughout the valley that surrounds the Great Enclosure are the ruins of many smaller stone enclosures and traces of more *daga* huts. These structures are the youngest and archaeologists speculate that they were built to accommodate the swelling population of Great Zimbabwe as its power and wealth drew in greater and greater numbers. At its height, the population may have reached 17–19,000, equivalent to that of medieval London. One of the enclosures is thought to have been where the wives of the *mambo* lived – there may have been up to 1,000 of them.

The layout of the site is reflective of sociopolitical attitudes. The physical separation and elevation of the Hill Complex mirrored and demonstrated the status of the king, while lesser chiefs of the kingdom maintained smaller enclosures of their own on less elevated points and the common people spread around the valley. When the population was at its height, Great Zimbabwe would have been a busy metropolis, with traders bringing in raw materials. The function of the Great Enclosure itself, however, remains something of a mystery. It is thought that it may have been a royal palace or played a role in initiation rites and/or religious ceremonies.

KING SOLOMON'S MINES

The city began to diminish from the mid–late 15th century, probably because the gold fields that underpinned its wealth began to run dry, but possibly also because the area could not support the environmental demands – particularly firewood and grazing – of the population. It was almost entirely deserted by the time that European explorers began to penetrate the interior of the continent, although subsequently there may have been low-level reoccupation of parts of the site and the Great Enclosure was probably still used for religious ceremonies.

The first Europeans to report the existence of the site were the Portuguese, who had set up trading forts on the East African coast to access gold, ivory and the other riches of the continent, but who did not penetrate inland. The Portuguese and subsequent Europeans connected Monomotapa with the legendary Ophir,

▼ **Outer Wall.** A 55-metre (180-foot) long alley runs between the inner and outer walls of the Great Enclosure. Its function is unclear, but it is likely that it was used for defensive purposes.

said in the Bible to be the home of the Queen of Sheba and the location of the gold mines that were the source of King Solomon's fabulous wealth.

By the mid-19th century, European explorers and missionaries finally penetrated the interior. In 1870, eccentric German explorer Karl Mauch heard tales of Monomotapa from a missionary and determined to win glory – and possibly riches – as the discoverer of Ophir. After various tribulations he reached the site, but alas for Mauch, a search of the site revealed neither gold nor gemstones, while his discoveries were greeted with relative indifference back in Europe.

WHITEWASH

At the end of the 19th century, the land around Zimbabwe fell into the hands of Cecil Rhodes, whose project for a British-dominated Africa required certain basic ideological and anthropological assumptions, namely that Africans were barbarous savages incapable of civilization

and that it was the 'white man's burden' to lift them out of their benighted state.

In subsequent decades, the area became the country of Rhodesia and Great Zimbabwe became an ideological battleground. For the white elite governing Rhodesia, it was important that the ruins should have a non-African background, and eccentric theories were put forward linking the ruins to the Vikings, pharaohs and the Lost Tribes of Israel. However, as early as 1905, the archaeologist David Randall-MacIver compared finds at the site with the prevalent use of identical artefacts and technology by the Shona peoples still living in the area. He drew the obvious conclusion: Great Zimbabwe had been built by Africans, probably by essentially the same people that still lived there.

Today Great Zimbabwe remains a politically charged place; a national monument that helps to define Zimbabwe's cultural identity, but also a focus of grievances over the nation's troubled colonial history.

ⓘ information

Location

Great Zimbabwe
Masvingo
Zimbabwe

 Travel site
www.encounter.co.za/article
/81.html

Transport

 Harare

 Masvingo

SOUTH ASIA & THE FAR EAST

This section features cities dating back to the dawn of civilization in South Asia (in the 3rd millennium BCE) and those that flourished in the Middle Ages, reflecting the breadth of cultures in the region. Despite obvious differences, there are also parallels between cities as widely separated in time and space as Harappa in the Indus Valley and Fujiwara-kyo in Japan.

Harappa and its sister city Mohenjo-daro were truly lost cities – in the sense that no one knew or remembered that they or the cultures that had given birth to them had ever existed. Locals knew of the great mounds that contained the remnants of the cities, but there was no way for them to know what the mounds represented. Instead they wove folk tales and fairy stories around them, telling of dancing troupes of little people atop the mounds. Only in the 20th century did the existence become apparent of a major centre of early civilization to rank alongside Mesopotamia or Ancient Egypt. By contrast, Fujiwara-kyo was a comparative latecomer to the world stage, founded some 3,500 years after Harappa. Like the Indus Valley city, it represented its region's first experiment in urbanism, for it was the first genuine city to be constructed in Japan.

Angkor, in Cambodia, grew more organically, but came to outdo in magnificence and size any city in the Far East. Historically, it is much closer to the modern era but it is in some ways far different from modern expectations of a city than the much more ancient Indus Valley cities. The modern urbanite may relate to the blocks of multi-storey brick buildings and the canyon-like streets of Harappa, but Angkor appears to lack common dwellings, palaces or government buildings. All that is left is a collection of temples.

Angkor. The capital of the Khmer Empire from the 9th to the 15th centuries CE, ▶
Angkor is perhaps the greatest religious complex ever constructed. When European explorers first encountered it in the 16th century it lay buried beneath thick jungle .

HARAPPA

See map p.7 (18)

LOCATION:	INDUS VALLEY, PAKISTAN
CONSTRUCTED:	*c.*2800BCE
ABANDONED:	*c.*1500BCE
BUILT BY:	INDUS CIVILIZATION – ALSO KNOWN AS HARAPPANS
KEY FEATURES:	MUNICIPAL PLUMBING; STREET GRID; BEADS, SEALS, PLAQUES, WEIGHTS, FIGURINES; LACK OF MONUMENTAL OR PUBLIC ART

Harappa and its sister city Mohenjo-daro (see pages 130) are two of the largest cities of the Indus civilization, also known as the Harappan civilization. The explorer Charles Masson, the first European to report the ruins of Harappa after stumbling upon them in the late 1820s, assumed it was the stronghold of King Porus, defeated by Alexander the Great in 326BCE.

In 1875, the first of a series of strange seals engraved with an unknown script was discovered at Harappa, pointing to the possibility that the mound concealed the remains of an entirely new civilization. This theory was confirmed by the 1924 Archaeological Survey of India, which announced the first results of excavations at Harappa and Mohenjo-daro.

The construction of the Lahore–Multan railway line through the area in the 1850s had already caused catastrophic damage to the site, however. Workers had used large quantities of bricks from the mounds as a ready source of ballast. Despite this, archaeologists have been able to construct a picture of the civilization that was centred on large urban settlements such as Harappa.

The roots of the Indus civilization date back as far as 7000BCE, when villages in the Indus Valley and the adjacent hill country marking the border between the Indian subcontinent and the Iranian region first developed. From about 4300–3200BCE (the Chalcolithic Era or Copper Age), these villages grew both larger and more influential throughout the Indus Valley region.

Ancient Harappa city walls. The wealth of brick masonry left at Harappa demonstrates why ▶ the 19th-century workers on the railway viewed the ruins as a rich quarry for ballast material.

THE IMPORTANCE OF BEADS

Excavations at Harappa show stone beads from every level of occupation and the production of finely wrought and often extremely difficult to make beads from rare and valuable materials is one of the defining technologies of the civilization. Figurines from the city show people wearing multiple strings of beads. There may have been a sophisticated 'language' of bead jewellery signalling social status, wealth, power and other attributes. They were also an export commodity. The most common material was steatite, also known as soapstone, but other materials included bronze, carnelian, agate and jasper. The harder the material and the smaller the bead, the more difficult it was to make. Excavations at Harappa suggest that different workshops in the city, perhaps under the direction of wealthy patrons, competed to advance their skills. Harappans also developed technologies for glazing and colouring beads, including the technology of faience, where a ceramic or stone is glazed with a lustrous sheen, particularly to make it look like lapis lazuli or turquoise, precious materials that stained easily when worn next to the skin. Later Harappans developed glass beads c.1700BCE, 200 years before the Egyptians first made glass.

From *c*.3700–2800BCE villages began to develop along the Ravi River, one of the tributaries of the Indus. This period saw the spread of a homogeneous culture through the region: toy models of bullock carts attested to the growth of trade routes that already reached for hundreds of kilometres and there was a spread of specialized craft technologies involving metalwork, pottery and jewellery (later central to the Indus civilization). At this time, the region may have experienced stronger seasonal variation in temperature – the flood plains and surrounding areas providing rich hunting and fishing, as well as fertile arable land. Precursors to a full-blown writing system began to appear, in the form of symbols inscribed onto pottery.

From 2800–2600BCE, Harappa grew into a large town, covering more than 25 hectares (61¼ acres) in two walled zones. Crafts, trade and social organization all became increasingly developed. By 2600BCE, the fully urban Harappan phase (or the Indus civilization) began and for 700 years Harappa dominated the surrounding region. At its height, it had a population of up to 80,000 people that covered over 150 hectares (370½ acres) with a circumference of more than 5 kilometres (3 miles).

Materials found in Harappa attest to a trade network that stretched from Central Asia to Mesopotamia and Arabia. The Harappans developed sophisticated systems for regulating trade, ownership and transactions. Seals with standardized symbols and a form of hieroglyphic writing known as the 'Indus script' were widespread, and it is thought they were probably used to mark goods with quantities and ownership. Similarly, marked copper plaques may have been the start of a system of currency, while small tokens of faience and fired steatite (soapstone) inscribed with marks may have been used for accounting purposes. Tablets of clay or faience were found snapped in half, and may have been used in transactions, with each party retaining half of the tablet until it was completed. Small stone cubes of graduated sizes were also used as standardized weights to ensure fair transactions in the trade of high-value merchandise, such as jewellery.

The city comprised three main walled areas and surrounding walled suburbs. Massive walls of mud brick, with brick gateways, served multiples purposes: control of access into the city, defence and also protection from floods. It was laid out on a grid system not seen again until the Greek cities of the mid-1st millennium BCE, with wide central avenues and regular-shaped buildings. It featured a water infrastructure of a scale and sophistication not seen anywhere else until Roman times. Numerous brick-lined wells scattered around the city provided a steady supply of water, while houses were equipped with bathrooms and latrines, which emptied into sewage drains, themselves connected to municipal main sewers.

It is hard to identify any remaining buildings as palaces or temples, although one of the main zones is described as a 'citadel', and each walled area probably had some public, administrative or religious function. The absence of the normal signs of authority (ie: of a king or emperor) is part of the wider enigma concerning the Indus civilization. How did it come to control such a wide area and how was it governed? It is possible that rather than government via a centralized monarchy, each city was ruled by its own elite class, who possibly combined religious and secular authority.

---

information

Location
Southern Punjab
North-east Pakistan

 Ancient Wisdom site
www.ancient-wisdom.co.uk/
pakistanharrapa.htm

Transport
 Lahore

 Harappa

MOHENJO-DARO

See map p.7 (19)

LOCATION:	INDUS VALLEY, PAKISTAN
CONSTRUCTED:	c.2600BCE
ABANDONED:	c.1500BCE
BUILT BY:	INDUS CIVILIZATION (HARAPPANS)
KEY FEATURES:	CITADEL; LOWER TOWN; PLUMBING; GREAT BATH; GREAT HALL; ASSEMBLY HALL; BEADS; SEALS; PLAQUES; WEIGHTS; FIGURINES

On the banks of the Indus, about 402 kilometres (250 miles) upstream from the ocean in the Sindh state of Pakistan, lie the remains of Mohenjo-daro (also known as 'Mound of the Dead'). The largest and best known of the cities of the Indus civilization, it survived beneath its mounds until the 20th century, when wholesale excavation revealed an almost intact brick-built metropolis with lanes and streets sandwiched between towering walls. However today the remains of the great city are under severe threat of crumbling into dust.

Although the earliest detected period of occupation at the site dates back to 3500BCE, the main phase of occupation began in 2600BCE and lasted for another 700 years, during which time the city dominated the southern Indus plain. The total area of the site is over 250 hectares (617 acres), but the heart of the city is split into a Citadel and an adjoining 80-hectare (198-acre) Lower Town, a pattern seen in many of the larger Indus Valley settlements. Almost all of the city is made of kiln-fired bricks, manufactured in huge quantities to standardized dimensions with the ratio 1:2:4.

Today the great mounds left by the city rise up to 12 metres (39¼ feet) above the surrounding flood plain – in ancient times they were even higher. Where as today the Indus flows to the east of the city, threatening at times to wash chunks of it away, in ancient times it flowed to the west and the city was strategically positioned between it and the Saraswati, another great river to the east, today extinct.

◀ **The Citadel at Mohenjo-daro.** The site escaped the destruction of railway workers, and its structures survived in far better condition that its sister city Harappa.

MOHENJO-DARO IN PERIL

Having lasted intact for thousands of years, Mohenjo-daro is now at severe risk. Exposure to the elements, flood waters from the Indus and poorly controlled salinity in the soils of the region, exacerbated by wasteful irrigation techniques, threaten to eat away at the bricks of the ancient city. Some of the oldest excavated areas have already crumbled into dust. Pakistani- and UNESCO-supported projects have spent millions of dollars on conservation and research, but so far have not been successful in preserving the city. The solution long proposed by archaeologists has been to rebury most of the city and only leave a small area exposed for tourists. At present, the Government of Pakistan's Department of Archaeology has experimented with partial reburial and intensive conservation that has seen some positive results. Future plans at Mohenjo-daro include extensive coring and a subsurface survey of the surrounding area to find the true limits of the site, followed by selective excavations to better understand the chronology of the settlement. In the course of new excavations at Mohenjo-daro and Harappa, as well as the many sites being excavated in other regions of Pakistan and India, it is possible that many mysteries of this civilization will gradually be revealed.

CITADEL AND LOWER TOWN

Of the two main areas, the large western mound concealed what is now called the Citadel (or the Acropolis). This was built up over hundreds of years, with mud brick platforms for houses and surrounding city walls that have now eroded away. Several major buildings have been excavated in the Citadel. Their exact roles are unclear – presumably they were public buildings but were they religious, royal or corporate? A large colonnaded building contains a specially engineered tank or pool, 12 metres (39¼ feet) long, 7 metres (23 feet) wide and up to 2.4 metres (7¾ feet) deep, known as the Great Bath. It was waterproofed with bitumen and was designed to be easy to empty and clean. It is possible that this might have been for ritual cleansing.

A massive structure with narrow hypocaust-like passages in its floor sits next to it, which was originally identified as a hammam or hot-air bath. Later it was believed to be the State Granary, where the grain tribute was stored on the basis that the passages were ventilation shafts. There is no concrete evidence for this, however. The more conservative label is the Great Hall. Other major buildings are known as the Assembly Hall and the College or Seminary, on the basis that it was the priest's quarters.

A collection of slightly smaller mounds to the east comprises the Lower Town.

▲ **Buddhist Stupa.** This structure was built atop the mound of Mohenjo-daro in the Kushan era (c. 100–250CE)

Each mound may have represented a walled neighbourhood (although as at Harappa the walls are more likely to have been for control of access or flood defences than fortifications).

Gridlike streets are oriented to the cardinal directions, with main avenues up to 10 metres (33 feet) wide and smaller streets separating city blocks that measure around 370 x 250 metres (404½ x 273½ yards) each. Over 700 wells may have supplied the city with water, while each house had bathing areas that fed into covered drains running beneath the streets. The wells remain intact to this day. Houses generally had at least two storeys and were designed to minimize dust and noise from the crowded streets.

The original scholarly interpretation of the Citadel–Lower Town divide was that the different mounds represented distinct functional sectors: the Citadel was the administrative sector, while the eastern mounds were industrial and residential. It is now thought that these functions shifted between districts over time and that all the areas show evidence of residential and industrial uses at different periods, perhaps representing shifting prosperity or jockeying for political power between districts.

ANOTHER BRICK IN THE WALL

Archaeologists and historians have traditionally been rather sniffy about the aesthetics and by extension the culture and spirit of the Indus civilization, as represented by Mohenjo-daro. No public or large-scale art has been found here; nothing proclaiming military might, imperial glory or even simply urban exuberance. Almost all of the arts and crafts objects that have been recovered are small – e.g. beads, votive figurines, clay and steatite seals and tablets. The symbols, motifs and styles represented are remarkably homogeneous across all the Indus civilization sites, prompting scholars to dismiss the culture of this ancient society as displaying

▼ **Seals.** Thousands of small steatite seals, probably used in trade, were discovered at Mohenjo-daro.

'a dead level of bourgeois mediocrity'. The monotony of Mohenjo-daro's endless brick vistas, which leave the impression of a giant termite mound now bereft of its teeming life, make it hard to disagree.

There are intriguing suggestions from arts and crafts recovered at Mohenjo-daro that the exuberance of later Hindu/ Buddhist aesthetics has its roots in its ancient precursor society. The most famous Indus Valley artefact, a steatite bust of a bearded figure wearing a diadem, usually interpreted as a priest–king, displays a zenlike serenity, while a common figure seen on seals and tablets is of a seated male in a lotuslike yogic position. Archaeologists working on Indus sites in Pakistan today draw parallels between modern-day *sang* festivals (annual spring fairs) and the fairs that their excavations show probably visited the same sites, and that were celebrated in the same way, 4,500 years ago.

THE DECLINE

Traditionalists believe that Mohenjo-daro and other cities were abandoned in around 1750–1500BCE, as the culmination of a general decline of the Indus civilization finished off by the Aryan invasion – the influx of Indo–European peoples recorded in the ancient Rig Veda, which tells of the god Indra helping his people to overcome mighty forts and ancient castles.

The discovery of some groups of skeletons at the city, some with apparent signs of violence and others in attitudes suggesting an escape attempt, lent weight to this attempt to link the ancient Vedic accounts with modern-day archaeological finds, just as Schliemann tried to do for Homer and Troy. Today there is considerable doubt over whether there ever was an Indo–Aryan 'invasion'. A more considered view of the archaeological record shows that occupation continued at Mohenjo-daro and other sites long beyond 1500BCE. It is considered unlikely that the city was ever fully abandoned due to its favourable position high above the floods.

The city did undoubtedly decline. During the late phase of occupation, from 1900BCE, there is evidence that it became increasingly crowded and that social order and central control broke down. For example, cuboid weights, inscribed seals and tablets, distinctive pottery marked with Indus script and raw materials and trade goods – all the indicators of a functioning, well-ordered culture – seem to disappear. There were probably multiple causes for this decline, including major changes to the Indus and Saraswati rivers. The latter dried up, driving the large numbers of people who had depended on it to seek aid and sustenance elsewhere; this may have contributed to overcrowding in Mohenjo-daro. The Indus also changed course, damaging the city and disrupting its agricultural base. These riverine changes may have been linked to wider ecological problems – the industrial-scale brick production of Indus Valley cities, together with that of other industries, consumed vast quantities of wood, which in turn may have led to deforestation and consequent climate changes.

In any event, a new social order emerged with new technologies, such as the use of the horse and iron. New languages and religion arose that can be linked to Vedic and early Hindu, Jain and Buddhist culture.

 ## information

Location
Sindh Province
Indus River
Pakistan

 Ancient Wisdom site
www.ancient-wisdom.co.uk/
Pakistanmohenjo.htm

Transport
 Moenjo Daro

ANGKOR

See map p.7 ⟨20⟩

LOCATION:	CAMBODIA
CONSTRUCTED:	802CE
ABANDONED:	LARGELY ABANDONED BY 1431CE
BUILT BY:	KHMER EMPIRE
KEY FEATURES:	ANGKOR WAT; ANGKOR THOM; BAYON TEMPLE; BARAY (RESERVOIRS); LACK OF NON-SACRED BUILDINGS

The great legacy of the Khmer Empire and arguably the greatest religious complex of all time, Angkor is a remarkable collection of temples and canals. It was buried under thick jungle when it was first encountered by European explorers. Recent investigations have revealed its full extent and provided valuable clues about the self-inflicted environmental problems that may have caused its demise.

'Angkor' is a Khmer word derived from the Sanskrit term for 'holy city'. It was the capital and religious centre of the Khmer Empire, a state that flourished in Indochina from the 9th to the 15th centuries CE. West of the Mekong River, near Tonle Sap – the largest lake in Indochina – on a wide, low-lying plain in the centre of modern-day

Cambodia, Angkor grew over the centuries into the largest pre-industrial city in history, with a population that may have numbered as many as a million. However, to the modern visitor there is little that resembles a city, just a collection of temples and water features widely scattered around a scrubby plain interrupted by patches of thick jungle.

SEAT OF THE KHMER GOD–KINGS

The region of Indochina known today as Cambodia was a collection of small states known to its northern neighbours, the Chinese, as Zhenla. At the start of the 9th century CE the Khmer king Jayavarman II, ruler of Kambuja, united the fragmented principalities of the region, extending his power over most of Indochina. In 802CE

Bayon Temple. Located in the middle of Angkor Thom and built by Jayavarman II, the Bayon is one of ▶ Cambodia's most famous temples. Its 54 towers are adorned by over 200 enigmatic stone faces.

▲ **Angkor Wat.** The colossal temple, viewed from across the wide moat that surrounds it. The moat symbolizes the oceans, and the towers the peaks of sacred Mount Meru, the abode of the Hindu gods.

he declared himself to be *devajara*, meaning 'royal god' – or a 'god–king' and establishing the royal personality cult as the central strategy by which the monarchy legitimized its rule – a strategy that was to lead to the incredible sacred architecture of Angkor.

In 889CE Yasovarman I moved the capital of the Khmer Empire to Angkor and set about transforming it into a sacred landscape: a replica of heaven on Earth. In the mythology of Hinduism, the state religion of the Khmers, the centre of heaven was Mount Meru, the abode of the gods, which was surrounded by the oceans. On Phnom Bakheng, the only natural hill in the area, the King built a pyramidal temple, symbolizing and recreating Mount Meru, in which sacred stone, or *lingam,* represented Shiva, one of the most important Hindu gods but also the Khmer god–king. Thus the Khmer god–kings gave physical expression to their divine right to rule.

To complete the earthly reconstruction of the cosmology, the temple at Phnom

Bakheng was surrounded by a moat, to represent the oceans, and this was fed from the first of two huge reservoirs, or baray, constructed at the site. The Eastern Baray is 7.5 x 1.8 kilometres (5 x 1 miles) in area and held up to 37 million cubic metres (48,400,000 cubic yards) of water; the Western Baray is even larger. They were the largest manifestation of the massive and complex system of irrigation channels, canals, moats and ponds – over a thousand of them – that underpinned life in Angkor. With this network of water-management features the Khmer were able to tame the annual flooding of Tonle Sap, irrigating their rice paddies and making their agriculture highly productive. A 13th-century Chinese visitor to Angkor recorded that they could produce three or four crops of rice a year, making it possible to support a huge population spread across a vast urban sprawl. Between 1992 and 2007, researchers were able to show that at its height Angkor had covered 1,000 square kilometres (386 square miles), making it the largest pre-industrial city in history. The next biggest rival, the Mayan city of Tikal was more than an order of magnitude smaller at 100–150 square kilometres (38½–58 square miles).

Angkor's glory years came in the 11th to 13th centuries. Under Suryavarman I (r. 1011–1050), the imperial palace–city of Angkor Thom began to take shape as a sort of capital within the capital. Suryavarman II (r. 1113–1150) built Angkor Wat, the most famous and the greatest of the temples at Angkor as his mausoleum. According to an inscription in the temple, he won the throne after slaying a rival prince in battle, leaping onto his war elephant and engaging him in single combat. Like the earlier temples, Angkor Wat with its five towers was a version of the sacred Mount Meru, which according to the myth had five peaks.

The greatest of the Khmer kings and the last great builder at Angkor was Jayavarman VII (r. 1181–1220), who refurbished Angkor Thom, built temples to his parents, and, on adopting Mahayana Buddhism as his personal faith, constructed the Buddhist temple of Bayon in the heart of Angkor Thom. It is famous for the giant faces peering out from its towers, representing Jayavarman VII as the *bodhisattva* Avalokiteshvara.

ZHOU DAGUAN

In 1296, a Chinese diplomat, Zhou Daguan, visited Kambuja and wrote an account of life in Angkor, *A Record of the Customs of Cambodia*. He depicted a society governed both by pervasive religious devotion and the strict and oppressive hierarchies that fed off that devotion to maintain their status.

Life in Kambuja was easier than in China, with the result that there was a significant population of Chinese. The first thing that such a new arrival had to do, Zhou Daguan reported, was obtain a wife, because trade was an exclusively female preserve. The typical Kambujan home was apparently devoid of furniture and many of the implements and utensils they used were made from leaves and were thus disposable.

Building in stone was reserved for the residences of the gods; secular buildings were made from more perishable materials, which did not long survive the abandonment of the city thanks to the tropical climate.

▼ **Ta Prohm Temple.** This temple at Angkor has been enveloped by the giant roots of a banyan tree.

LOSS AND REDISCOVERY

After Jayavarman VII's death there was a brief return to Hinduism. Eventually Buddhism was established as the state religion of the Khmers and many of the temples were converted to Buddhist shrines. There was also a general decline in the Khmer Empire and from the late 13th century it was threatened by the growing power of the Thai (or Siamese) kingdom to the west. According to the popular history of the site, the end of Angkor came in 1431, when the Thai invaded the western provinces of Kambuja and sacked the city, at which point the Khmer fled to the new Khmer capital near Phnom Penh.

Historians have largely discredited this, and substantial populations continued into the 16th century, possibly as lay support for communities of Buddhist monks based in the temples. The centre of political gravity had shifted irrevocably and Angkor became a shadow of its former self. By the 17th century, the population had declined substantially. In the tropical heat and humidity the jungle reclaimed the site; the roots of fig trees and other plants wreaking considerable damage on the unmortared masonry, forcing blocks apart and threatening to bring down the temples.

The extraordinary ruins of Angkor first became famous in Europe thanks to the writings and sketches of French explorer Henri Mahout, who visited the site in

Although the Portuguese described Angkor in the 1550 it is Mahout's account that catapulted Angkor to fame as an archetypal lost city, although the wonder and awe it provoked was not limited to Europeans. Siamese scribes, writing just two centuries after the fall of the Khmer Empire, recorded that 'angels from heaven came to help in building this magnificent city'.

WHY DID IT DECLINE?

It is generally accepted that Angkor was in terminal decline by the 15th century. One theory is that the Khmer regime was exhausted both by continual warfare and by the tremendous demands of the monumental labour that had created Angkor's sacred landscape. Towards the end of the Khmer era, the state religion also became Theravada Buddhism and George Coedès, perhaps the foremost scholar on Angkor, argues that this form of the religion, with its emphasis on the denial of the reality of the individual, was not compatible with the cult of royal personality and this combined with the military and economic exhaustion of the state resulted in an erosion of central authority. That in turn led to a breakdown of maintenance of the irrigation system, with knock-on effects for the agricultural basis of the city's existence.

Angkor's water-management system has also come in for closer scrutiny. The recent project to map the full extent of the ancient city has led to claims that its vast urban sprawl became self-defeating. Mass deforestation to meet population demands and constant construction projects led to soil erosion, while the water-management system became too large to be effective, resulting in the irrigation canals becaming clogged with silt and ceasing to function. Archaeologists from the University of Sydney also believe that the transition from the medieval warm period to the Little Ice Age may have been the trigger for the city's water crisis. The breakdown of the irrigation system may also have led to stagnant water and an explosion of malaria-carrying mosquitoes.

Today, the encroaching jungle, looters, art thieves and increasing tourism are among the factors contributing to Angkor's decline.

---

information

Location

Angkor Archaeological Park
Siem Reap
Cambodia

 Sacred Destinations site
www.sacred-destinations.
com/cambodia/angkor-wat

Transport

✈ Siem Reap

FUJIWARA-KYO

See map p.7 (21)

LOCATION:	ASUKA, JAPAN
CONSTRUCTED:	682CE
ABANDONED:	710CE
BUILT BY:	EMPEROR TENMU AND EMPRESS JITO
KEY FEATURES:	IMPERIAL PALACE; HALLS OF STATE; IMPERIAL AUDIENCE HALL; SUZAKU-MON; CERAMIC ROOFING; YAKUSHIJI TEMPLE; WOODEN TABLETS/COINS

Construction at Fujiwara-kyo, effectively Japan's first city, was only begun around 682CE. The builders produced an impressive and well-planned city dominated by a huge imperial palace complex that included the largest building Japan had ever seen. The construction of Fujiwara-kyo, also Japan's first permanent capital, marked and facilitated the transition of Japan from a disparate group of competing chiefdoms to a nation state.

SHORT-LIVED CAPITAL

Construction of the city was begun during the reign of the Emperor Tenmu. A site in the Asuka region was chosen – a plain between three hills in the present day Takadono district of Kashihara-shi, where three of Japan's main roads converged: the Nakatsumichi, Shimotsumichi and Yoko-oji, which were to mark the east, west and north boundaries of the city, respectively. The location had originally been known as Fujiigahara, or 'plain of the wisteria well'; this was shortened to simply Fujiwara, 'wisteria plain' and so the city became Fujiwara-kyo, 'city of the wisteria plain'. Canals were dug to allow timber and stone to be brought to the site (although these were later filled in before the city was actually occupied).

Tenmu's death in 687 brought a temporary halt to construction, but the project was continued under his widow, the Empress Jito, and finally completed in 694, whereupon Fujiwara-kyo served as her capital.

Fujiwara-kyo was the capital of Jito's successors, the Emperor Mommu and the

◀ **Yakushiji Temple.** Several Buddhist temples were constructed near the imperial palace. The Yakushiji Temple still exists, having been moved to a new site at Nara, but most of it is a reconstruction.

Empress Gemmei, but in 710 the capital was relocated 14.5 kilometres (9 miles) north, to Nara. Fujiwara-kyo was stripped of all recyclable materials and what remained may have been further devastated by a fire in 711. By the 9th century, the site had largely returned to farmland; it was not definitively rediscovered until excavations began in 1934.

CHINESE MODEL CITY

The city was laid out according to the *jobo* grid system, like a Go board, along the lines of Chinese cities like the Tang capital of Changan. Although it could not compete with Chinese metropolises for size, recent excavations have revealed that it may have covered as much as 25 square kilometres (9¾ square miles), considerably bigger than traditionally believed. The city was divided by orthogonal *oji*, or avenues, into 12 *jo* (north–south blocks) and 8 *bo* (east–west blocks). It was at Fujiwara-kyo that the Japanese custom began of dividing the capital into a *sakyo* ('left capital') and *ukyo* ('right capital') along a north–south dividing line. Whereas in later capitals the city blocks were delineated by numbers, at Fujiwara-kyo each block had its own name – e.g. Ohari-machi and Hayashi-mach.

As many as 30,000 people may have lived here. A document called the *Shoku Nihongi* records that in 704, 1,505 households in Fujiwara-kyo received bolts of cloth. Household registers (known as *koseki*) from the era – a device introduced as part of the *ritsuryo* system to help keep track of taxpayers – show that each household numbered on average more than 16 people, suggesting a minimum population for the city of at least 24,000.

The focal point of the city was the Fujiwara-no-miya, the imperial palace. Like a Chinese palace this was actually a compound or complex of walls, plazas and buildings. Sited in the central north zone of the city, so that the monarch could symbolically look south to survey his dominions, the palace was approximately 1 square kilometre (⅓ square mile) and was surrounded by a 5-metre (16½-feet) wide outer ditch, wooden walls about 5 metres (16½ feet) high and then another, inner ditch. There were three principal gates; the main one, the Suzaku-mon, was in the south wall. It led to the heart of the complex: the Dairi, the emperor's personal residence and the Chodoin, the Halls of State, of which the most important was the Daigokuden, the Imperial Audience Hall. At 45 metres (147½ feet) wide, 21 metres (69 feet) deep and 25 metres (82 feet) high, this was the largest building in Japan. The *omiya dodan*, or 'earth platform of the great palace' upon which the Daigokuden rested, still rises above the surrounding plain at the site.

Significantly the Audience Hall and other palace buildings were the first in Japan to be roofed with ceramic tiles – another innovation from China. It is estimated that up to two million tiles were used on the palace.

Around the palace were the mansions of aristocrats and high-ranking officials. One such mansion near the Suzaku-mon covered 12,000 square metres (129,166 square feet). Lesser bureaucrats and commoners lived further out. There were also several Buddhist temples in the city. One of them, Yakushiji, still exists, having been moved along with the capital to the new site at Nara, where it still stands today (although most of it has been reconstructed at one point or another).

Just as the city itself was an innovation, so its construction and habitation involved other innovations. Fujiwara-kyo saw the first latrines yet found in Japan. Analysis of their contents shows that the inhabitants ate raw vegetables and undercooked fish, such as carp and trout, which gave them worms. To help regulate and facilitate trade, the city also saw the first coins ever minted in Japan. In 1999, archaeologists found a cache of Fuhonsen coins, named for the two *kanji* characters on the front – *fu* and *hon* meaning 'wealth' and 'basis', thought to be a reference to a legendary Chinese epigram, 'the basis for wealth of the people is food and money'. These coins, dating from the late 7th century and predating the previous earliest known Japanese coins of 708, are thought to represent another stage in the Taika Reform project to modernize Japan, transforming it into a nation state along Chinese lines.

In the end, the relocation of the capital from Fujiwara-kyo was probably down to political/symbolic reasons, with the new location intended to provide an even larger and more impressive backdrop to the new system of government, one which was not associated with the traditional ruling region of Asuka (Nara was slightly further to the north). Historian Hisashi Kano also suggests that geomancy – landscape magic – may have played a part: the hill directly to the south of Fujiwara-kyo effectively disrupting the feng shui of the palace.

(i) information

Location

Asuka-Fujiwara
Nara Prefecture, Japan

 Asuka Park site

www.asuka-park.go.jp
/asuka_en/index.html

Transport

 Kansai

THE AMERICAS

In the Americas lie perhaps the archetypal lost cities: temples, palaces and pyramids that rear up out of virgin jungle, with only weird petroglyphs to hint at the nature of the cultures that once dwelt there. Cities such as those of the Maya and the Inca, where a combination of circumstances – the swift and total destruction of indigenous civilizations and cultures, the remoteness of the sites and the rate at which the rainforest encroaches – conspired to allow them to disappear from human ken. The tales of their rediscovery are equally the stuff of romantic legend, with intrepid explorers hacking through the jungle in search of lost cities of gold.

Other pre-Columbian civilizations left their mark on the Americas, from the mound builders of Mississippi and the canyon-dwelling Pueblo peoples of the southern deserts to the Aztec Empire of Mexico and the mysterious ancient Tiwanaku culture of the Andes. In many cases, the remains left by these kingdoms and empires are relatively young, compared to the ancient sites of the Old World, and are therefore in good enough repair to amaze and enthral visitors even today.

From the point of view of the historian, New World civilizations offer a unique opportunity. Unlike in the Old World, where civilizations inevitably developed in the context of a network of influences, the New World civilizations developed in glorious isolation. The similarities and differences between these lost cities and those of the Old World are instructive and they offer valuable insights into the importance of ecology, the fragility of the environment in the face of urban civilization and the world views of exotic cultures. Perhaps it is this last feature that adds to the allure of the lost cities of the Americas – the religion and mysticism of their builders are both strange and intriguing, lending an extra layer of mystery to the already enigmatic.

Machu Picchu. Perhaps the ultimate lost city, Machu Picchu is sited high in the Peruvian Andes and is a ▶ profoundly mysterious site. Its isolation suggests that it was a personal retreat for the Inca and his family.

CAHOKIA

See map p.6

LOCATION:	COLLINSVILLE, ILLINOIS, NEAR ST LOUIS, MISSOURI, USA
CONSTRUCTED:	C.1050CE
ABANDONED:	C.1350CE
BUILT BY:	MISSISSIPPIAN CULTURE
KEY FEATURES:	MOUNDS; MONKS MOUND; GRAND PLAZA; WOODHENGE; PALISADE

In the centre of the American Midwest a collection of man-made mounds mark the site of North America's greatest pre-Columbian city. Huge earthworks and vast landscaped plazas testify to the existence of a well-organized and sophisticated society, but its legacy seems to have vanished almost without a trace.

This Illinois State Historic Site encompasses some 70 mounds, including the enormous Monks Mound, which has a base larger than that of the Great Pyramid at Giza. The site today covers around 890 hectares (2,200 acres), but in its heyday, around 1100CE, the city had an area of 1,619 hectares (4,000 acres) and a population that may have numbered 10,000–20,000 people.

While it is known that the city appeared almost within a generation, it is not known why this remarkable development occurred nor why it was subsequently abandoned.

OVERNIGHT SENSATION

The flood plain known as the American Bottom offered rich arable land that could be cultivated even without heavy ploughs, and Neolithic peoples there grew crops such as sunflowers and squashes. In the 1st millennium CE the cultivation of corn spread north from Mesoamerica, triggering population growth and the emergence of the formative stages of a recognizable Mississippian culture a little before 1000CE. In around 1050CE, the city at Cahokia sprang into existence over a relatively short time, in what some archaeologists have described as a 'big bang' moment.

Monks Mound. This is the largest of the 70 man-made earthworks at Cahokia. ▶

CHUNGKE

Plazas were probably used for playing chungke, a game still practised by Native Americans today. It involves a stone disc, which is rolled down the centre of a court, while the players throw javelin-like sticks, either to knock over the disc or to see who can land nearest to where it comes to a halt. Players were known to wager all their worldly goods, down to the shirts off their backs, on the game of chungke. In Mound 72 at Cahokia, 15 chungke stones were found as part of a tribute cache to an early Cahokia leader.

Cahokia was the ultimate embodiment of the characteristics that mark out the Mississippian culture, including large communal plazas; massive mounds, especially flat-topped ones; wooden palisades; characteristic styles and motifs on pottery; the game of chungke (see above) and the practice of human sacrifice.

CITY OF MOUNDS AND PLAZAS

Mounds at Cahokia came in three main types and each one probably served a different function. Platform or flat-topped mounds, such as Monks, usually had buildings on top of them. Cone-shaped or round-topped mounds were used for burials, while ridge-topped mounds may have served as landmarks or boundary markers, and also appear to have had mortuary functions. The greatest mound – known as Monks Mound because in 1811 when it was first described by an antiquarian there was a community of Trappist monks living nearby – is over 30 metres (98½ feet) high with a base measuring approximately 300 x 240 metres (984 x 787 feet), one-quarter larger than the base of the Great Pyramid. It has several different terraces and platforms and a flat top where a huge wooden building once sat – possibly the residence of the paramount chief or a temple. Monks Mound was constructed over several centuries, with new layers added periodically, perhaps to mark the death of a leader and the ascension of a new one. It has been estimated that to build it took 15 million baskets of earth deposited over 300 years. The earth came from what are known as borrow pits, some of which are still visible at the site.

To the west of Monks Mound stood a 'woodhenge' – a circle of cedar posts, used as a solar calculator to determine the timing of equinoxes and solstices. It was rebuilt several times, possibly to take into account the successive enlargements of Monks Mound, the profile of which it was aligned with. This woodhenge suggests that the plazas and pyramids of the Mississippians were part of a solar cult.

THE END OF CAHOKIA

Many theories have been advanced to explain the decline and abandonment of Cahokia. Overpopulation may have stretched the ability of the surrounding area to feed the city. The high population and its consumption of wood may have led to deforestation, loss of biodiversity, soil erosion, flooding and rising water levels. Climate change, such as the cooling associated with the Little Ice Age from *c.*1250, may also have played a part. Increased warfare and conflict suggests that political changes were taking place, and perhaps challenges to Cahokia's authority. And if a settlement the size of Cahokia was unusual in Mississippian culture, perhaps it is not so surprising that once it declined, the population subsided back to a scattered, village-centred existence.

Cahokia declined in the 13th century, and it was essentially abandoned by the late 14th century. The Mississippian culture lived on in the south-eastern USA, however, and it is thought likely that the Natchez Indians of Mississippi – described by Spanish and French explorers in the 16th to 18th centuries – may have been the inheritors of the Mississippian tradition. They lived in palisaded villages, played chungke, practised human sacrifice (attested to by headless skeletons interred alongside nobles in burial mounds) and followed a solar religion.

Cahokia itself, however, attracted little attention and is still comparatively unknown. The mounds were treated with little respect by early settlers who flattened them to clear farmland, and even today much of Cahokia is unprotected. There was also a trend among historians and archaeologists to deny or disparage the achievements of the Mississippians, with the mounds attributed to mythical pre-Columbian Europeans such as Phoenician or Welsh settlers, in keeping with the Manifest Destiny agenda that legitimized the dispossession of the indigenous peoples because of their 'primitive' nature.

ⓘ information

Location

Cahokia Mounds
30 Ramey Street
Collinsville
Illinois 62234

 Sacred Destinations site
www.sacred-destinations.com
/usa/cahokia

Transport

 Chicago

PUEBLOS OF CHACO CANYON

See map p.6 (23)

LOCATION:	NEW MEXICO, USA
CONSTRUCTED:	c.10TH CENTURY CE
ABANDONED:	LATE 12TH CENTURY CE
BUILT BY:	ANCESTRAL/ANCIENT PUEBLO PEOPLES (ALSO KNOWN AS ANASAZI)
KEY FEATURES:	GREAT HOUSES; PUEBLO BONITO; KIVAS (CEREMONIAL CHAMBERS); TURQUOISE BEADS; ROAD SYSTEM

The desert canyons of the South-west USA are deeply inhospitable. Today they support only a meagre population at an extremely low density, yet somehow this same area supported several complex societies centred on communities that may have numbered 10,000 or more. These communities vanished before Columbus, leaving the empty remnants of the largest buildings in pre-Columbian America. These buildings are known as Great Houses, and are the grandest form of pueblo, or village, constructed by the pre-Columbian inhabitants of the area. Although they are popularly known as the Anasazi, from the Navajo word for 'ancient ones', the Navajo themselves were post-Columbian immigrants to the area, and archaeologists and historians now prefer to refer to the prehistoric residents as the Ancient Pueblo Peoples, or, in reference to their latter-day descendants the Hopi and Zuni, the Ancestral Pueblo.

RISE OF THE PUEBLO PEOPLES

At its height, Chaco Canyon was a thriving population hub centred on Pueblo Bonito and 12 other Great Houses along the canyon, spaced at intervals of about a mile. Holes in the canyon's northern walls, drilled for wooden roof beams, show that much of its length was lined with houses, while the

◄ **Kivas.** The circular kivas found at Chaco Canyon seem to be identical to those constructed by Native Americans and it has been assumed that they were used for the same purpose – for ritual and tribal gatherings.

remains of hundreds of small settlements have been found on the canyon's southern side. Taken together with the size of Great Houses like Pueblo Bonito (see right), this would seem to indicate that up to 10,000 or more people lived here. On the other hand, the consensus among most archaeologists is that even with the Anasazi's expertise at dry-land agriculture, the meagre natural resources of the region would have limited the maximum population to less than 5,000 and this would appear to be borne out by the finding that many of the rooms in Pueblo Bonito were unoccupied for long stretches of time. One suggestion is that the Great Houses were ceremonial centres that were only periodically occupied.

Chaco Canyon was also the hub of a sophisticated network of roads that linked it to tens of thousands of smaller Anasazi settlements across the Four Corners region; 22,000 have been identified in New Mexico alone. The roads are up to 96 kilometres (59½ miles) long and 13 metres (42½ feet) wide and some still show evidence of stone kerbs, indicating that they were carefully constructed and maintained. The presence of trade goods at Pueblo Bonito shows that these roads were used to import food, timber and other raw materials, particularly luxury goods such as turquoise, shells and even exotic bird feathers from as far away as Mexico.

PUEBLO BONITO

The jewel in the Anasazi crown was the Great House at Pueblo Bonito. This was the biggest Anasazi structure. It was up to six storeys high and comprised over 600 rooms, all jumbled together into a contiguous structure not dissimilar to Çatalhöyük (see page 16), with entrance to upper levels via flat roofs, which themselves were the site of communal activities. It was built with timber roof supports made from huge single logs up to 5 metres (16 feet) long, weighing as much as 317.5 kilograms (700 pounds). Over 200,000 of them were used in the construction of the Chaco Canyon pueblos, which took shape over the course of two centuries. At first, pinyon pines from the local area were used, but when these were exhausted the Anasazi had to look further afield. Analysis of mineral isotopes in surviving timbers has allowed experts to determine the exact locations these logs came from – the Chuska and San Mateo mountains, around 80.5 kilometres (50 miles) away. The Anasazi had no carts or pack animals, so they would have had to bring the logs down from the mountains by muscle power alone. The timber, well preserved in the dry desert air, has also helped archaeologists to date the settlements through the science of dendrochronology – counting tree rings to determine dates.

▲ **Pueblo Bonito Great House in Chaco Canyon.** This building was the biggest Anasazi structure and would have been up to six-storeys high and comprised more than 600 rooms.

Most of the rooms in Pueblo Bonito are around 4 x 5 metres (13 x 16 feet), but there are several large circular chambers called 'kivas' after contemporary Native American structures that seem to be identical. Contemporary kivas are used for rituals and tribal gatherings and it is assumed that Anasazi kivas served similar functions. Other rooms in the pueblo were food-storage chambers, while beneath the floors of some rooms were burials complete with grave goods, including great quantities of valuable turquoise beads. The skeletons of those buried here are taller and larger than at lesser Anasazi sites, suggesting that the well-fed elite lived in the Great Houses.

SEEDS OF DESTRUCTION

Two of the greatest mysteries regarding Chaco Canyon and the Anasazi are how they supported a dense population in such a barren region and why their civilization collapsed. The two are probably closely linked. The upland desert of the Four Corners region appears to be highly unsuitable for agriculture. Rainfall is low and tends to occur in sudden intense bursts that cause flash flooding where most of the run-off is lost. Temperatures at high elevations, where rainfall is higher, are very low and the conditions mean that forest growth and soil fertility replenishment are slow.

The Anasazi used several techniques to overcome the limits of the environment. They devised sophisticated water management schemes in Chaco Canyon, damming the main canyon and feeder canyons to catch and store run-off. They grew crops at sites such as the alluvial bottom of Chaco Canyon where the water table was close enough to the surface for the roots of their crops to reach and they

▼ **Mesa Verde.** This is the largest cliff dwelling in North America. Like Chaco Canyon, Mesa Verde was an important population centre for the Ancestral Pueblo.

founded agricultural stations over a wide area so that at least some of them would garner enough rainfall to produce a surplus big enough for redistribution.

But in the success of the Chaco Canyon Anasazi lay the seeds of their downfall. Their system of agriculture was marginal – in good years, with decent rainfall, it could support a large population, but they could only store corn for two years (after this it will rot and become inedible), making them vulnerable to drought. At the same time, the urban model they adopted at Chaco Canyon was unsustainable in this impoverished ecosystem. Analysis of plant remains in packrat middens (nests of dried litter, which can survive for thousands of years in the desert, left by packrats) has shown that after 1000CE the Chaco Canyon Anasazi had deforested the local area, which in turn led to problems with soil erosion and loss of fertility. Eventually Chaco Canyon became a largely unproductive centre, dependent on the rest of the wider Anasazi world to supply it with everything from food and timber to luxury goods.

By the 12th century the growing environmental problems caused by the dense population combined with a prolonged drought period caused the collapse of the Chaco Canyon Anasazi. Dendrochronology shows that the last timber used at Pueblo Bonito was cut in 1117, while the youngest anywhere in the Canyon dates to 1170. Other Anasazi sites show evidence of fortification, warfare and cannibalism, and it seems likely that as crops failed and famine spread, the centre could not hold and the society descended into disorder and warfare. Some of the Anasazi appear to have survived by moving to new areas and the lack of useful artefacts at many Anasazi sites shows that the residents effected a planned evacuation. It is believed that the Pueblo Peoples, including the Hopi, Zuni and Acoma, who still live in pueblos and practice dry-land agriculture, are at least partly descended from the Anasazi.

ⓘ information

Location

Chaco Culture National
Historic Park
Nageezi
New Mexico

 Chaco Park site
www.nps.gov/chcu/index.htm

Transport

✈ Albuquerque

TENOCHTITLÁN

See map p.6 (24)

LOCATION:	VALLEY OF MEXICO, MEXICO
CONSTRUCTED:	1325CE
ABANDONED:	1521
BUILT BY:	AZTECS
KEY FEATURES:	MAIN TEMPLE PYRAMIDS; CANALS AND CAUSEWAYS; GREAT MARKET; AQUEDUCTS; PUBLIC LATRINES; CHINAMPAS 'FLOATING FIELDS'

When Hernán Cortés and his small band of conquistadors first saw the Aztec capital of Tenochtitlán, they were astonished. Bernal Diaz del Castillo, one of Cortés's soldiers, wrote that, 'It was all so wonderful that I do not know how to describe this first glimpse of things never heard of, seen, or dreamed of before.' But just two years later all this would be gone, razed to the ground after a desperate and bitter siege.

TENOCHTITLÁN AT ITS PEAK

At first the city grew organically and haphazardly, but after a major flood the Mexica took the opportunity to rebuild along carefully planned lines, perhaps inspired by the ruins of ancient Teotihuacán

to the north-east. The new city was laid out on a grid, with four main processional ways dividing it into quarters, which themselves were divided into smaller neighbourhoods called *calpulli*. Each *calpulli* had its own local temples and markets, and was organized around a tightly knit hierarchy of family and clan networks. The fifth district of the city, reflecting the fifth cardinal direction that the Mesoamericans recognized, was the centre, where heaven and Earth came together at a sort of *axis mundi* (offering clear parallels with ancient Babylon – see page 58).

Here the Mexica constructed a great sacred precinct, surrounded by a wall of carved serpents, 347.5 x 301.75 metres (380 x 330 yards) in area and with room for

Plaza de las Tres Culturas in Mexico City. This area displays the architectural styles of three cultural ▶ strands – the Aztec remains a pyramid–temple; the Spanish Church of Santiago from the early 17th century; and the modern building for the Department of Foreign Affairs.

▲ **Templo Mayor.** Human sacrifices would have been made at the top of the pyramid and the bodies then thrown down the staircase. Two serpent heads guard the foot of staircase.

more than 8,000 people. Within stood huge stone pyramids, including the Main Temple. About 27 metres (more than 90 feet) high, the Main Temple consisted of two stepped pyramids side by side on a huge platform. They symbolized the two sacred mountains of Aztec myth; the homes of the two central deities of their pantheon. The southern pyramid was sacred to Huitzilopochtli ('Hummingbird Left') and represented Coatepec, or Snake Mountain. The northern pyramid symbolized Tonacatepetl, the Edenic fertile mountain paradise home of Tlaloc

('Long Cave'), the god of fertility that the Aztecs had appropriated from the Toltecs. Thus, like the Khmer at Angkor Wat (see page 136), the Mexica had transformed the heart of their capital into a sacred landscape, affirming their claim to dominion.

The rise to power of the Aztecs was accompanied by a remarkable population explosion in and around the Valley of Mexico. In the early Aztec period (1150–1350CE) the Valley had a population of c.175,000. By the late Aztec period (1350–1519CE) it had increased to nearly a million, with around 200,000 people living in Tenochtitlán alone, making it one of the largest cities in the world at the time. According to the Spanish, who were welcomed, albeit warily, to the city and initially viewed it as awestruck tourists, the great market in the city attracted crowds of up to 60,000 people – more people than lived in the biggest city in Spain. Here they observed women taking an equal part in many aspects of life, including trading; gaudily made-up prostitutes loudly chewing a form of gum to attract customers; humble commoners; haughty warriors and priests and an astonishing profusion of food and other goods from across America, including seafood from both the Pacific and Atlantic coasts, exotic animals and birds from the jungles to the south, obsidian blades from the north and possibly even goods from the Inca Empire to the far south.

The Spaniards were also struck by the cleanliness of the city. Aqueducts brought fresh water to the city and the residents bathed at least once a day. There were no pack animals to foul the streets and each house was equipped with private latrines.

DOWNFALL

To the Spanish, the Aztecs' culture of bloodletting and human sacrifice was wrong, and their hostility was inflamed by their lust for gold. They moved into the palace as 'honoured guests', but in reality they made the Aztec emperor, Moctezuma, their virtual prisoner, and issued increasingly strident demands for lavish gifts of gold. Tenochtitlán rapidly became a powder keg, which was ignited when Cortés' lieutenant, Pedro de Alvarado, had hundreds of Aztec nobles massacred. The Indians rose up in revolt and the Spaniards made a desperate night flit. However, Cortés returned a year later with an army of Spanish soldiers and levelled the city. Today the site of Tenochtitlán lies at the heart of Mexico City and the Valley of Mexico once again hosts one of the largest cities on Earth.

 ## information

Location

Templo Mayor
Zocalo
Mexico City
Mexico

 ### Travel site

www.differentworld.com/mexico/areas/mexico-city/guide-zocalo.htm

Transport

 Mexico City

CHICHEN ITZA

See map p.6 (25)

LOCATION:	YUCATÁN PENINSULA, MEXICO
CONSTRUCTED:	c.600CE
ABANDONED:	1000 OR 1250CE
BUILT BY:	MAYA
KEY FEATURES:	SACRED CENOTE; EL CASTILLO; EL CARACOL; HIGH PRIEST'S TEMPLE; CASA DEL MONJAS; GREAT BALL COURT; CHAC MOOL STATUES

The greatest city of the northern Maya, located in Mexico's Yucatán peninsula, Chichen Itza is today one of the most famous and most visited of their ancient relics. It is celebrated for its pyramids, its Great Ball Court and for the brooding Sacred Cenote, or water-filled sinkhole, into which human sacrifices were flung to intercede with the subterranean gods. The Cenote made Chichen Itza a site of religious importance and pilgrimage long after its collapse.

A SOPHISTICATED CULTURE

The Maya were the most sophisticated pre-Columbian culture in the Americas, the only one with a fully-developed system of writing, along with all the other characteristics shared by Mesoamerican civilizations, such as monumental architecture, advanced astronomy and mathematics and highly developed water management.

Chichen Itza itself became a significant city sometime around 600CE and the architectural styles it displays suggest a mixed heritage of Mayan and other influences, including 'Mexican' ones (i.e. from the Valley of Mexico, where pre-Aztec civilizations such as the Toltecs were coeval with the Maya). According to the *Chilam Balam*, a history written by Mayan sources after the Spanish conquest had begun, the city took its name from a group of 'foreigners' known as the Itza, who spoke only a broken version of Maya. It is thought that this might be a reference to a group known as the Chontal Maya from areas to

◄ **Chac Mool.** These statues at Chichen Itza are reclining figures with their heads turned to one side holding dishes for offerings in their laps.

the west, in the modern Mexican states of Tabasco and Campeche, who spoke a different dialect of Maya. They would have had contact with Mexican cultures and hence could have introduced these influences to Chichen Itza.

The city rose to further prominence in the 9th century and became the leading power of what is known as the Late Classic period. This does not necessarily mean that it was the capital of a Mayan empire, because the lack of pack animals and the limitations of Mayan agriculture tended to restrict the military reach of Mayan city states, so that the control of any one king could not extend much further than his own power base. But Chichen Itza was the dominant force in the region, its authority possibly bolstered by the prestige of its Sacred Cenote.

After two centuries of this hegemony, it lost control after a civil war, recorded in the Mayan chronicles, which eventually led to the razing of the city in around 1250CE,

▼ **El Castillo (The Castle).** Also known as the Temple of Kukulcan, the Feathered Serpent. Large crowds gather here on the spring and autumnal equinoxes to watch the Sun cast serpentine shadows across the northern face of the pyramid.

testified to by the burned remnants of some
of the temples atop its pyramids.

THE SACRED CENOTE

The key to Chichen Itza's power was
its cenotes. The northern lowlands of
Yucatán can be arid, with rainfall coming
intermittently and unpredictably (and often
destructively, in the form of hurricanes),
and no rivers or streams of any sort. The
strange geology of the region, with porous
and easily eroded karst limestone, which
is low-lying and thus very close to the
water table, means, however, that water
is accessible through the cenotes and these
supplied the Maya with water and made
it possible to support sizeable populations
in an otherwise inhospitable region.

The Sacred Cenote is a particularly
large example. It is almost perfectly circular,
with a diameter of more than 50 metres
(164 feet) and a 20-metre (65½-feet) drop
to the murky green water, which itself is
at least 15 metres (49 feet) deep, with a
bottom of thick slime and mud. Chroniclers
of the post-Columbian era recorded that the
Maya would make offerings and sacrifices
to the rain god Chaac, hoping that they
would intercede with him and gain his
favour. In particular, they would throw
in young maidens. Sometimes several
would be tossed in at dawn and any who
survived until midday would be hauled

out and interrogated about what they had
seen, relating lurid stories of their exchanges
with those who dwelt in the black depths
of the well.

Inspired by these tales, in 1894
Edward Thompson, the American consul
in the nearby town of Merida, purchased
the land on which Chichen Itza's ruins stood
and determined to make a remarkable
investigation of the depths of the Sacred
Cenote. He brought in dredging equipment
and spent years scooping foul muck from its
bottom, having calculated the correct spot
to explore by throwing corpse-sized logs
from the rim to see where they landed and
sank. He successfully brought up a range
of artefacts, including spears, axe heads,
copper discs, pottery and votive offerings
such as jade ornaments and small gold
bells. The ornaments had been deliberately
broken and the bells flattened, perhaps as a
way of symbolically 'killing' them. He also
brought up large numbers of balls of copal
incense, which was burned during sacrifices,
and the bones of many young women and
other victims.

BUILDINGS OF CHICHEN ITZA

Chichen Itza has an 'old town', known as
Old Chichen, where temples and structures
are located, but the most impressive ruins
(many of them restored) are in the newer
city. It is dominated by the great stepped

▲ **El Caracol (The Snail):** This round building sits on a square platform and is named after the spiral stone staircase that winds up the interior of the building. It was used as an observatory by the Maya.

pyramid of Kukulcan, known as El Castillo ('The Castle'). A stairway runs up each of the four sides, climbing up nine platforms to a height of 25 metres (82 feet). The pyramid is aligned so that at the spring equinox the corner of the pyramid casts a snakelike shadow onto its northern face, which 'slithers' as the Sun progresses across the sky (attracting huge crowds of tourists). Buried within is another, older pyramid, with a chamber within containing a jaguar-shaped throne and a Chac Mool statue.

A smaller but similar pyramid is known as the High Priest's Temple, because when Thompson investigated it he found what he took to be the burial chamber of a priest. In fact he found a descending series of burial chambers, starting at the top of the pyramid. Sounding the floor with a steel rod he detected a void beneath and pried up the flagstone, accessing another chamber. He repeated this through five tombs until he penetrated a space carved into the rock below the pyramid, which was full of ash and heat-fused jade beads. In an evocative passage he describes what happened when he lifted a slab in the corner of this chamber, expecting to find only a heap of ashes beneath: 'It yielded so suddenly that I fell back with it… My companions also fell back, for it disclosed a big, circular, pitch-black hole… [from which] came a… cold, damp wind… The two natives [his companions] were simply glued to their places in sheer terror. Finally Pedro spoke. "It is the mouth of Hell."' In fact it was a 15.25-metre (50-foot) deep pit, and in true Indiana Jones style, Thompson had himself lowered into it to discover that it was crawling with toxic spiders guarding a collection of mortuary artefacts.

Other important buildings are the Temple of the Warriors, a stepped pyramid with rows of carved columns showing warriors, similar to Toltec structures at the city of Tula. A building known as La Casa del Monjas ('the nunnery') because it was thought to have been a sort of convent for an order of priestesses and female initiates,

but which is now understood to have been a governmental building. To the north of this is El Caracol ('The Snail'), a round building on a square platform named for the spiral stone staircase that winds up the interior of the building. It resembles a modern-day observatory and indeed was used for this purpose by the Maya.

To the north-west of the castle is the Great Ball Court, the largest such court ever discovered. It is 175 metres (574 feet) long and 70 metres (229½ feet) wide, making it bigger than an American football field, and has 7-metre (23-feet) high walls along each side, decorated with carvings of teams of players, including a grisly depiction of what happened to the losers of the Mesoamerican ball game. This was played with a heavy ball of rubber, which players kept aloft with their forearms, hips and thighs, possibly with the aim of scoring through hoops, two of which are set into the tops of the court's side walls. In one of the carvings, the captain of the defeated team is shown decapitated, with jets of blood spurting from his neck.

ⓘ information

Location

Chichen Itza
Yucatán
Mexico

 **Travel site**

www.chichenitza.com

Transport

 Merida

TIKAL

See map p.6 (26)

LOCATION:	GUATEMALA
CONSTRUCTED:	*c.*200BCE
ABANDONED:	*c.*900CE
BUILT BY:	MAYA
KEY FEATURES:	GREAT PLAZA; MANY STEPPED PYRAMIDS; BALL COURTS; PALACES; STELAE

The largest and greatest Maya city, Tikal was so utterly abandoned that it was not fully rediscovered until 1848. Yet more than 60,000 people – perhaps up to 200,000 – lived in a city that covered over 121.75 square kilometres (47 square miles), and which dominated the Mayan heartland from the Yucatán to western Honduras. Only recently has decipherment of the mysterious Mayan script made it possible to read the wealth of inscriptions (known as 'glyphs') at the site, revealing the city's bloody history of violence and intrigue.

The name by which Tikal is known today is a relatively recent appellation, meaning 'at the waterhole', a reference to the semi-artificial reservoirs the ancient Maya constructed to help control their water supply. According to the glyphs at the site, the city's inhabitants called it Yax Mutul, and the glyph for *mutul*, thought to represent a top-knot of hair, itself probably symbolic of a sacred corn sheaf, has been found on stones in cities throughout the region, testament to the city's long reach.

RISE AND FALL

The first settlement of Tikal dates back to 800BCE, but the city only properly began to take shape around 200BCE, with the laying down of Tikal's urban core, particularly what would become the Great Plaza. This was a large flat area covered in plaster, which remained the city's hub for a thousand years. Tikal's glory days coincided with the Classic period of Maya civilization,

Temple One on the Great Plaza. Facing west towards the setting Sun, Temple One was ▶
built during the Late Classic Period and was considered to be a portal to the underworld.

▲ **Stone mask.** This mask at the North Acropolis complex represents the principal Mayan bird deity.

from around 250–900CE. However, Maya writing long predates this, the first dated inscription at Tikal – indeed the first one found in the Maya heartland – dates to 292CE (or 8.12.14.13.15 in the Maya Long Count calendar). It is written on a *stela*, an inscribed upright slab of stone, of which dozens were erected at Tikal, with about 70 in the Great Plaza alone. These *stelae* and other inscriptions have enabled historians to piece together a very precisely dated list of kings and queens, in the process uncovering a tale of dynastic politics and

inter-city rivalry that saw Tikal become the pre-eminent Maya city. By controlling the lucrative trans-isthmus trade routes and through force of arms, Tikal dominated most of the Maya heartland.

The inscriptions show that one of Tikal's most revered rulers, Jaguar Paw died on 31 January, 378CE, on the same day that Siyah K'ak', a lord from the 'Mexican' city of Teotihuacán, arrived. It is hard to avoid the conclusion that 31 January 378 was the exact date of a battle in which Siyah K'ak', a conquering general from Teotihuacán, defeated and slew Jaguar Paw.

Tikal now fell under Teotihuacán influence, with Mexicanized architecture and the introduction of a military innovation, the spear-thrower. The long-term result was an increase in conflict with its neighbours, which eventually led to the establishment of an alliance between Tikal's enemies. Glyphs from Tikal and other sites enable us to trace the politics of this era in fine detail. It seems that its traditional enemy, the city state of Calakmul, was able to capitalize on a fatal misjudgement by the rulers of Tikal, who sprang a surprise raid on their erstwhile ally Caracol in 556CE. Nursing resentment, Caracol allied with Calakmul, and waited until a favourable astronomical alignment to begin its revenge. Caracol's sorcerer–priest–astronomers declared that the most auspicious moment was when Venus rose in its closest conjunction with the dawn Sun, which came to pass in 562CE. With Calakmul's help, Caracol launched a devastating raid on Tikal and in the decades that followed the Calakmul-Caracol axis cemented the suppression of Tikal by engineering alliances with other city states previously under Tikal's control. Finally, in the late 6th century, Calakmul supported a breakaway clique of Tikal nobles who set up a rival city at Dos Pilas, which called itself New Tikal.

By the late 6th century, Tikal was entirely ringed by hostile city-states, and for over a century no inscriptions were made there. This period of 'silence', known as the Tikal Hiatus, marks the transition from the Early to Late Classic period. When Tikal finally re-established itself, the nature of Maya culture had changed, with Teotihuacán elements expunged.

In 672CE, Tikal began its resurgence with a campaign against Dos Pilas and over the next 100 years Tikal regained much of its former power and reached the height of its magnificence. More and more grand buildings were erected on raised platforms around the city centre – more than 3,000 in total – including monstrous stepped pyramids up to 64 metres (210 feet) high. There are also numerous palaces (which may in fact be government buildings), ball courts, causeways, observatories and domestic buildings.

By 750CE Tikal was at its peak, but little more than a century later the city faced a catastrophic collapse. The last dated *stela* erected at Tikal is dated 869, while the last to be found anywhere in the southern lowlands dates to 909.

A HOSTILE ENVIRONMENT

Tikal's achievements were possible because of its burgeoning population, which seemed to defy the environment as it appears today.

Despite the lush forest that surrounds the city, the southern lowlands where Tikal is sited do not provide the most promising environment for the agricultural base needed to support an advanced civilization. Rainfall is highly variable, with long dry seasons, there are few rivers and, except in valley bottoms, the soils are thin and slow to replenish fertility. Tikal itself was so utterly abandoned that in 1525 when Hernán Cortés marched through the region, he passed unaware within a few kilometres of the city. In 1841, during their survey of dozens of Mayan sites, pioneering explorers John Lloyd Stephens and Frederick Catherwood missed it entirely. So how was it possible for a city of over 60,000 people to have existed here a thousand years earlier?

At Tikal the Maya sought to overcome these limitations by adapting natural depressions and excavating new ones to create massive reservoirs – big enough to hold enough drinking water to meet the needs of 10,000 people for up to 18 months. They also adopted agricultural innovations, such as mulching to preserve moisture and fertilize fields, multiple cropping in a single year and timing the

▼ **Temples I, II and III.** The view from Temple IV at Tikal.

planting of crops to make maximum use of heavy rains and floods. Intensive agriculture produced high yields and they were able to support steadily increasing population densities of up to 580 people per square kilometre (1,500 per square mile), For comparison, this is twice that of the most densely populated countries in Africa today.

But this drive to maximize the intensity and productivity of their agriculture put the Maya on a collision course with nature. Although the relatively scarce valley bottoms of the southern lowlands could maintain a reasonable level of fertility, the marginal zones that the Maya increasingly looked to exploit could not. With population growth came additional pressures on the environment. Forest clearance for agriculture was exacerbated by wood cutting for construction, firewood and the production of plaster, with which the Maya were obsessed (they used it as a means of beautifying their edifices). Deforestation led to soil erosion, flash floods, loss of water retention and eventually to climate change through reduced rainfall. Replenishment of soil fertility collapsed and the population was forced to rely on the overextended core arable land of the valley bottoms.

Proxy climate records, such as sediments deposited in lake beds, reveal that this period also saw one of the most severe and extended dry periods for over a thousand years, with particular peaks in drought conditions around 810, 860 and 910CE. Environmental breakdown had probably already led to tension over diminishing land and food resources, and the severe droughts plunged the Classic Maya into a catastrophic collapse. Authority broke down, conflict raged and millions starved. The archaeological evidence shows that palaces and government buildings at Tikal were burned and it is not hard to imagine a vengeful populace turning on the rulers whose covenant with their people was to ensure prosperity in return for obeisance. By the end of the 10th century, what was the greatest American metropolis of its age had been completely abandoned.

(i) information

Location

Tikal

Guatemala

 Sacred Destinations site

www.sacred-destinations.com/guatemala/tikal

Transport

 Flores

TIWANAKU

See map p.6 (27)

LOCATION:	LAKE TITICACA, BOLIVIA
CONSTRUCTED:	*c.*200CE
ABANDONED:	*c.*1000CE
BUILT BY:	TIWANAKU CIVILIZATION (AYMARA?)
KEY FEATURES:	GATEWAY OF THE SUN; AKAPANA PYRAMID; SEMI-SUBTERRANEAN TEMPLE; KALASASAYA TEMPLE

From around 200CE to around 1000 Tiwanaku was the centre of a major civilization, which spread its influence across a broad swathe of the Andean region, as far as southern Peru, northern Chile and even Argentina. They left impressive monuments of stone and earth, including pyramids, temples, colossal statues and *stelae*. At 3,850 metres (12,631 feet) above sea level, it may have been the highest capital city in history.

CHALLENGES

The high plateau between the western and eastern ranges of the Andes is known as the Altiplano. After the Himalayan plateau, it is the highest plain on Earth and Lake Titicaca, formed because several rivers drain into the plateau and have no access to the sea, is the highest navigable lake on the planet. There is a harsh dry season and in the wet season rains can be torrential. The lakes are very shallow and fluctuate wildly in size with seasonal floods. Temperatures vary greatly both diurnally and annually, and the high altitude and thin air exacerbate all these issues. Only a limited range of crops can be grown and yields may be very low.

The ancient people of Tiwanaku developed a number of highly successful solutions to these challenges. Slopes were terraced so that they could be farmed without fields being washed away. Networks of canals irrigated areas that would otherwise be too dry. Animal husbandry developed large herds of camelids such as llamas and alpacas, with guinea pigs reared

◀ **The entrance to the Kalasasaya Temple.** As seen from the Semi-subterranean Temple, looking towards the Ponce Monolith (also known as El Fraile, or 'The Friar').

inside homes to provide extra sources of protein. But the crucial development was raised-field agriculture, known as *suka kollus* by the local Aymara people. In areas with rich soil but that are normally susceptible to flooding, small fields are raised above the level of the plain using soil dug from canals that run between them. The water in the canals acts as a heat buffer, absorbing heat from the Sun during the day and then slowly releasing it overnight to create a microclimate for the fields, protecting them from otherwise deadly frost. Edible fish are also raised in the canals and the sludge from fish droppings and decaying vegetation is dredged out and used to fertilize the fields along with camelid dung. This intensive form of agriculture allowed the Tiwanaku to grow crops that would not otherwise be viable.

Thanks to these advances the population in the Tiwanaku region flourished. Estimates reach as high as 1.4 million, with up to 60,000 thought to have lived within the 6 square kilometres (2⅓ square miles) of

▼ **The Kalasasaya (walled temple).** This was the sacred centre of the city, where the emperors were buried.

central Tiwanaku and more than 50,000 in satellite settlements.

CITY OF STONE

The site of Tiwanaku became the dominant city of the Altiplano from around 500CE until its collapse in around 1000CE. During this time, the Tiwanaku constructed a number of impressive stone monuments. To construct these monuments they practised the most sophisticated dry-stone masonry yet discovered. Large stones were shaped to fit together so perfectly that a razor blade cannot be inserted between them. Irregular stones rather than square ones were used, probably to make the masonry more earthquake proof, and in some places I-shaped copper bars were used to fasten the stones together for added protection. Many blocks were decorated with carvings, including faces and giant figures, while other monoliths and *stelae* have earned the site the nickname of 'the Stonehenge of the New World'.

The greatest structure at Tiwanaku was the Akapana, a 17-metre (55¾-feet) high terraced hill with a 61-square metre (656-square feet) base. At the summit a 15.25-square metre (164-square feet) sunken court with the marks of rectangular rooms may have hosted elite residents or been a temple. Burials of human remains, ritual objects and offerings have been found. A number of other temples are associated with the Akapana, most notably the Semi-subterranean and the Kalasasaya. The former is a sunken court with low walls studded with carved human heads. In the centre, surrounded by smaller *stelae*, is a massive *stela* known as the Bennett Monolith, after an archaeologist who did pioneering work at the site.

The Kalasasaya is a 130-metre (426½-feet) long platform constructed from sandstone blocks alternating with tall, upright stones, although this may not be how it originally looked. In a sunken court on the eastern side is a massive stone statue, known as the Ponce Monolith (after another archaeologist). Exciting recent work at this temple adds weight to the Stonehengelike identification of the site, because it seems that the Kalasasaya served as a remarkably accurate, self-correcting solar calendar. Subsurface radar has revealed a deep shaft at the site where the observer in this monumental observatory would have stood, so more revelations could be forthcoming.

Next to the temples were buildings that may have been residences for the elite, while underneath a patio in this part of the city, archaeologists have discovered the remains of several seated individuals, facing a man with a puma-decorated sacred pottery vessel. Many of the other carvings show figures holding *keros* – ceremonial goblets

▲ **The Gateway of the Sun.** Set within the Kalasasaya Temple, the portal is constructed of a single block of andesite. Archaeologists believe it may have been used as a calendar.

that were used to serve *chicha*, or corn beer. Also in this part of the city is Tiwanaku's most famous monument, the Gateway of the Sun, which is actually carved from a single piece of stone that must have been hauled to the site from over 40 kilometres (24¾ miles) away. The figure carved on the gateway is known as the Staff God, and although the Inca claimed it was their progenitor god Viracocha, it is not known who he really was or what he is holding. Even this titanic monument has been moved from its original position during reconstruction work.

The common people probably lived in residences around this central complex. The picture is unclear, but some archaeologists think that neighbourhoods may have been specialized by craft or other occupation.

EMPIRE OR CEREMONIAL CENTRE?
Distinctive Tiwanaku pottery styles have been found across a broad area of the Andean region and there is little doubt that its iconography and ideology had a profound impact on the region, with elements informing cultures up to the Inca.

But there is an ongoing debate about whether Tiwanaku was an empire. There is some evidence that it was more of a loose federation of smaller states called *ayllus*, rather than a monolithic empire.

AFTERLIFE OF TIWANAKU

The reasons for Tiwanaku's decline remain a mystery, but it is strongly suspected that a major drought may have been responsible. Even before the end, the evidence is that from around 800CE most new building in the area involved smaller rural settlements, and that after the main city was mostly abandoned there was continued settlement in the area in small rural villages, in a return to a pre-urban lifestyle.

But the story of Tiwanaku does not end there. When the Inca came upon the site in the course of their expansion and empire-building, they quickly co-opted it for ideological purposes. Its ancient ruins, clearly predating their own origins, challenged their propaganda, which predicated their right to rule on their 'most

ancient' status. To overcome this, they simply claimed the site as a legendary Inca homeland, identifying the Staff God on the Gateway of the Sun as their own creator deity Viracocha, and weaving Tiwanaku into their myths.

Four hundred years after the downfall of the Incas at the hands of the conquistadors, Tiwanaku again found itself co-opted as an ideological tool. This time it was by the Bolivian government, smarting from a damaging war with its neighbour Paraguay, and seeking a national identity to rival that of the Peruvians, who had the Inca. Accordingly the government settled on Tiwanaku, commissioning a clumsy reconstruction of its monuments and carting coachloads of schoolchildren to marvel at their national icons. Even today archaeologists studying the site have to negotiate the politics surrounding it, while at the same time racing against time to preserve the ruins from uncontrolled development and exploitation that has already done considerable damage and threatens their long-term survival.

 information

Location

Tiwanaku

Bolivia

 UNESCO site

www.unescoworldheritagesites
.com/tiwanaku_bolivia.htm

Transport

✈ La Paz

MACHU PICCHU

See map p.6 (28)

LOCATION:	PERUVIAN ANDES
CONSTRUCTED:	1440CE
ABANDONED:	c.1530CE
BUILT BY:	INCA
KEY FEATURES:	CASA DEL VIGILANTE (THE GUARD HOUSE); INTIHUATANA (HITCHING-POST OF THE SUN); MAIN TEMPLE; TEMPLE OF THE THREE WINDOWS

In 1911, American archaeologist Hiram Bingham was led up the steep path from the Urubamba Valley, deep within the Peruvian Andes, by local guides who had promised him something special. What he found was Machu Picchu, known today as the ultimate lost city and a profoundly mysterious site.

EMPEROR'S RETREAT

Machu Picchu was constructed 2,350 metres (7,709 feet) above sea level and lies about 70 kilometres (43½ miles) north-west of the old Inca capital of Cusco. Construction was probably begun by the Sapa Inca (High King) Pachacuti in around 1440CE, or possibly his successor Yupanqui.

The geographical and economic isolation of the site, away from the major Inca highways and equipped with so little agricultural terracing, points to the fact that Machu Picchu probably wasn't an important economic, military or administrative centre. Historians today consider that it was most likely a personal retreat for the Inca and his family, with spiritual and ceremonial functions at its heart.

SACRED SITE

Among the many mysteries of Machu Picchu is the question of why the emperor chose to build this remarkable complex in such an inaccessible and apparently unimportant spot. The solution is probably to be found in the link between landscape and spirituality that lay at the heart of Inca philosophy. The Inca revered natural

Lost city. Despite its relatively central location Machu Picchu was completely unknown to all but a few locals before the Spanish conquest in 1532. ▶

features such as peaks, stones, caves and springs as *apus*, ('shrines or sacred spots'), and Machu Picchu lies in the heart of a landscape rich in spiritual significance. Many of the major buildings of the site have been interpreted as temples and when the Inca was in residence there was probably a whole retinue of priests and astronomers who worked with the site to determine important solar events and perform ceremonies, rituals, sacrifices and prayers.

THE MACHU PICCHU SITE

Climbing up to Machu Picchu from the south-east, the visitor first passes through the agricultural sector, which consists of more than 100 terraces. Small stone huts called *collpa* dot the terraces – these were probably storehouses.

Approaching the urban sector, the visitor passes the Casa del Vigilante – the Guard House – which commands spectacular views of the city and the Urubamba Valley. A little further along, the trail passes through the main gate and into Machu Picchu proper, which has three main districts. The Residential District is where the simplest buildings are located, and is probably where the servants and workers of the citadel lived.

Across the Main Plaza from the Residential District, in the Sacred District, are a number of buildings that were probably temples. On a hill to one side

of the plaza is one of Machu Picchu's treasures, the Intihuatana, or Hitching-Post of the Sun, a large, carved and shaped rock that culminates in a roughly square upright pillar, believed to have played a central role in Inca solar rituals and calendar calculations. Other highlights of the Sacred District include the Main Temple and the deliberately roofless Temple of the Three Windows, with its characteristic trapezoid

▲ **Residential district.** These simple buildings are thought to have been the homes of the servants of the emperor.

windows (believed to offer greater stability against earthquakes).

The third district, between the Sacred District and the agricultural zone, is the Royal District, where it is believed higher-status people stayed. The buildings here are of fine stonework and have evocative names such as the House of the Wise and the Princesses' Bedrooms. Next to the Royal Palace is the Temple of the Sun, believed to

have been an astronomical observatory. The Temple of the Sun has a fountain built into its very fabric, highlighting the ingenious hydrological engineering of the Incas, who used aqueducts, shaped natural channels and natural springs in the area to supply the whole citadel with running water.

Also in this district are what is believed to be the jail and the Monumental Mausoleum, where mummies were stored

▲ **Temple of the Sun.** Once used as a solar observatory, this temple is the only circular building at Machu Picchu.

in niches cut into the walls and sacrifices may have been carried out. It is also believed that sacrifices or ritual torture may have been performed in the Temple of the Condor, a partly natural rock chamber that resembles the outstretched wings of a condor. Grooves in the rock that lead down into a pit were probably used for channelling blood. Similar grooves are found on altars and niches elsewhere in the city. The indications are that bloodletting and sacrifice were a major feature of life in Machu Picchu, as evidenced by discoveries of human bones bearing the marks of butchery.

MYSTERY

One of the great mysteries of Machu Picchu is a technical one. How could such an impressive scheme be realized in such a remote and inaccessible location, by a Bronze Age culture whose use of the wheel was restricted to children's toys? The answer is probably a combination of ingenuity, technical mastery of the arts of architecture, masonry and rock carving, and sheer manpower. In particular, the skill of the Incas is epitomized by their extraordinary dry-stone construction, in which dressed blocks of stone are fitted together without mortar, but with such precision that even the thinnest knife blade cannot be forced between them.

Perhaps the most haunting mystery of Machu Picchu is the enigma of how it came to be lost and what happened to the people who lived there. Archaeologists have unearthed about 200 skeletons of people buried on the site, but this is far fewer than the likely population of the city, suggesting that the inhabitants abandoned it or at the very least did not die off slowly enough to be buried.

The low number of burials suggests in fact that the city was not occupied for very long, being in use for only a few decades in total. In the centre of the citadel is a large quarry, where the stone for construction came from, and it appears to have been in full use when abandoned. Perhaps after years of struggling, it was decided that it was too costly to continue construction and maintenance of such a remote site.

Above all, however, the fact that knowledge of Machu Picchu was lost to all but a few locals is testament to the way in which Inca society collapsed in the face of the diseases and physical and cultural destruction the conquistadors visited upon them. A society with no formal written records (the Incas had no writing) relied on oral transmission and a continuity of scholarship for its cultural transmission and such education was restricted to a small elite. The impact of the Spanish conquest was too much for such a fragile system and it was all too easy for a remote city, far off the main highways along a difficult trail that would have been overrun by jungle within a year without maintenance, to fall off the map. But the Incas' tragedy is our blessing, for it means the lost city survived the ravages of the Spanish conquest.

THE FUTURE

There are now serious concerns about the future of Machu Picchu as the pressures of mass tourism are threatening the site. Its enduring mysteries may never be solved, but tragically they may outlast the site itself.

(i) information

Location

Machu Picchu

Peru

 Travel site

www.peru-machu-picchu.com/

Transport

 Cusco

 Aguas Calientes

RECOMMENDED READING

Atkinson, Austen, *Lost Civilizations: Rediscovering Ancient Sites Through New Technologies* (Watson-Guptill Publications, 2003)

Bahn, Paul (Ed), *Lost Cities: 50 Discoveries in World Archaeology* (Phoenix Illustrated, 1999)

Baudez, Claude and Picasso, Sydney, *Lost Cities of the Maya* (New Horizons, 1992)

Blegen, Carl William, *Troy and the Trojans* (Thames and Hudson, 1963)

Butterworth, Alex and Laurence, Ray, *Pompeii: The Living City* (Phoenix, 2006)

Cottrell, Leonard, *Lost Cities* (Robert Hale Ltd, 1957)

Curtis, J.E. and Tallis, Nigel (Eds), *Forgotten Empire: The World of Ancient Persia* (British Museum Press, 2005)

Diamond, Jared, *Collapse: How Societies Choose to Fail or Survive* (Allen Lane, 2005)

Dobbins, J.J. and Foss, P.W. (Eds), *The World of Pompeii* (Routledge, 2007)

Doumas, Christos, *Thera: Pompeii of the Ancient Aegean* (Thames and Hudson, 1983)

Fagan, Brian (Ed), *Discovery! Unearthing the New Treasures of Archaeology* (Thames and Hudson, 2007)

Guaitoli, Maria Teresa and Rambaldi, Simone, *Lost Cities From the Ancient World* (White Star, 2006)

Harrison, Peter D., *The Lords of Tikal: Rulers of an Ancient Maya City* (Thames and Hudson, 1999)

Jacques, Claude and Freeman, Michael, *Angkor: Cities and Temples* (River Books, 1997)

Kenoyer, Jonathan Mark, *Ancient Cities of the Indus Valley Civilization* (Oxford University Press, 1998)

Lane Fox, Robin, *The Classical World: An Epic History from Homer to Hadrian* (Allen Lane, 2005)

Leick, Gwendolyn, *Mesopotamia* (Penguin, 2002)

Levy, Joel, *Lost Histories* (Vision, 2006)

Levy, Joel, *The Atlas of Atlantis and Other Lost Civilisations* (Godsfield Press, 2007)

Macdonald, Colin F., *Knossos* (Folio Society, 2005)

Maqsood, Rosalyn, *Petra: A Traveller's Guide* (Garnet Publishing, 1996)

Jim Masselos (Ed), *The Great Empires of Asia* (Thames & Hudson, 2010)

Owens, E.J., *The City in the Greek and Roman World* (Routledge, 1992)

Stefoff, Rebecca, *Finding the Lost Cities: The Golden Age of Archaeology* (British Museum Press, 1997)

Tomlinson, R.A., *From Mycenae to Constantinople: Evolution of the Ancient City* (Routledge, 1992)

Various, *Mysteries of the Ancient Ones*, a special edition of *Scientific American* (2005)

INDEX

ACKNOWLEDGEMENTS

The author and publishers would like to extend their grateful thanks to the following for reading sections of the book and for offering their expert advice and guidance on the history of particular sites: Barry Baldwin, Gina Barnes, John J. Dobbins, Aidan Dodson, Damian Evans, Shahina Farid, Andrew George, Bill Iseminger, C.T. Keally, Jonathan Mark Kenoyer, Andreas Kropp, Matthew W. Stolper and Ken Wardle. Any errors that remain are entirely the responsibility of the author. The author would also like to thank Kate Parker, Charlotte Macey and Jolyon Goddard.

PICTURE CREDITS

Alamy: p.18 (Images & Stories), 20 (Images & Stories), 25 (Peter Horree), 30–31 (John Farnham), 32 (Wojciech Wójcik), 34 (Ali Kabas), 37 (DB Photography), 54, 56 (Robert Harding Picture Library Ltd.), 58 (INTERFOTO), 61 (Imagestate Media Partners Limited – Impact Photos), 65 (Robert Harding Picture Library Ltd.), 68 (The Art Archive), 72 (Bildarchiv Monheim GmbH.), 81, 82 (The Art Archive), 96–97 (MARKA), 100 (Jim Henderson), 103 (The Art Archive), 104 (Jim Henderson), 109 (Rolf Richardson), 114, 116 (Robert Harding Picture Library Ltd.), 120, 122 (Images of Africa Photobank), 130 (Robert Harding Picture Library Ltd.), 133 (Iconotec), 134 (Robert Harding Picture Library Ltd.), 138 (David Ball), 142 (MJ Photography), 147 (Tibor Bognar), 155 (David Muenker), 160 (John Mitchell), 162 (Russell Kord), 172 (Stefano Paterna), 176 (Ian Nellist), 178 (Alatom); Corbis: p.17 (Nathan Benn/Ottochrome), 22 (Yann Arthus-Bertrand), 66 (Chris Hellier), 170 (Diego Lezama Orezzoli); Fotolia: p.4 (Shirley), 38 (jokerpro), 41, 43 (bluetrue), 44 (Dario Bajurin), 46 (missbobbit), 49 (Konstantin Yolshin), 50 (sootra), 53 (Mischa Krumm), 62 (Patricia Hofmeester), 76–77 (Sadequl Hussain), 90 (Alex White), 95 (Denis Bachinskiy), 112 (urosr), 119 (Darren Patterson), 125 (globe-trotter), 137 (XtravaganT), 156 (maverick), 166 (Banauke), 174 (javarman), 182–183 (Alexander); Getty Images: p.107 (DEA/A. Dagli Orti), 127 (National Geographic), 159 (De Agostini), 169 (Kelly Chang Travel Photography); Pictures Colour Library: p.15 (Tony Hutchings); iStockphoto: p. 9 (onfilm), 10 (jlvphoto), 26 (MaxFX), 29 (richacno), 74 (Dhuss), 78 (gioadventures), 89 (Nsonic), 93 (stevenallan), 98 (Amanda Lewis), 140 (tbradford), 152 (P_Wei), 164 (kemie), 181 (alexeys), 184 (digital); Photolibrary: p.86 (Doug Pearson/Jon Arnold Travel), 149 (Peter Arnold Images/Jim Wark/Photolibrary); p.71 Troels Myrup Kristensen.